Customer Information Control System
Complete Self-Assessment Guide

The guidance in this Self-Assessment is based on Customer Information Control System best practices and standards in business process architecture, design and quality management. The guidance is also based on the professional judgment of the individual collaborators listed in the Acknowledgments.

Notice of rights

Trademarks

Table of Contents

About The Art of Service

The Art of Service, Business Process Architects since 2000, is dedicated to helping stakeholders achieve excellence.

Defining, designing, creating, and implementing a process to solve a stakeholders challenge or meet an objective is the most valuable role… In EVERY group, company, organization and department.

Unless you're talking a one-time, single-use project, there should be a process. Whether that process is managed and implemented by humans, AI, or a combination of the two, it needs to be designed by someone with a complex enough perspective to ask the right questions.

Someone capable of asking the right questions and step back and say, 'What are we really trying to accomplish here? And is there a different way to look at it?'

With The Art of Service's Standard Requirements Self-Assessments, we empower people who can do just that — whether their title is marketer, entrepreneur, manager, salesperson, consultant, Business Process Manager, executive assistant, IT Manager, CIO etc... —they are the people who rule the future. They are people who watch the process as it happens, and ask the right questions to make the process work better.

Contact us when you need any support with this Self-Assessment and any help with templates, blue-prints and examples of standard documents you might need:

http://theartofservice.com
service@theartofservice.com

Included Resources - how to access

Included with your purchase of the book is the Customer

Information Control System Self-Assessment Spreadsheet Dashboard which contains all questions and Self-Assessment areas and auto-generates insights, graphs, and project RACI planning - all with examples to get you started right away.

How? Simply send an email to
access@theartofservice.com
with this books' title in the subject to get the Customer Information Control System Self Assessment Tool right away.

You will receive the following contents with New and Updated specific criteria:

• The latest quick edition of the book in PDF

• The latest complete edition of the book in PDF, which criteria correspond to the criteria in...

• The Self-Assessment Excel Dashboard, and...

• Example pre-filled Self-Assessment Excel Dashboard to get familiar with results generation

• In-depth specific Checklists covering the topic

• Project management checklists and templates to assist with implementation

INCLUDES LIFETIME SELF ASSESSMENT UPDATES

Every self assessment comes with Lifetime Updates and Lifetime Free Updated Books. Lifetime Updates is an industry-first feature which allows you to receive verified self assessment updates, ensuring you always have the most accurate information at your fingertips.

Get it now- you will be glad you did - do it now, before you forget.

Send an email to **access@theartofservice.com** with this books' title in the subject to get the Customer Information Control System Self Assessment Tool right away.

Purpose of this Self-Assessment

This Self-Assessment has been developed to improve understanding of the requirements and elements of Customer Information Control System, based on best practices and standards in business process architecture, design and quality management.

It is designed to allow for a rapid Self-Assessment to determine how closely existing management practices and procedures correspond to the elements of the Self-Assessment.

The criteria of requirements and elements of Customer Information Control System have been rephrased in the format of a Self-Assessment questionnaire, with a seven-criterion scoring system, as explained in this document.

In this format, even with limited background knowledge of Customer Information Control System, a manager can quickly review existing operations to determine how they measure up to the standards. This in turn can serve as the starting point of a 'gap analysis' to identify management tools or system elements that might usefully be implemented in the organization to help improve overall performance.

How to use the Self-Assessment

On the following pages are a series of questions to identify to what extent your Customer Information Control System initiative is complete in comparison to the requirements set in standards.

To facilitate answering the questions, there is a space in front of each question to enter a score on a scale of '1' to '5'.

1 Strongly Disagree

2 Disagree

3 Neutral

4 Agree

5 Strongly Agree

Read the question and rate it with the following in front of mind:

'In my belief,
the answer to this question is clearly defined'.

There are two ways in which you can choose to interpret this statement;
1. how aware are you that the answer to the question is clearly defined
2. for more in-depth analysis you can choose to gather evidence and confirm the answer to the question. This obviously will take more time, most Self-Assessment users opt for the first way to interpret the question and dig deeper later on based on the outcome of the

overall Self-Assessment.

A score of '1' would mean that the answer is not clear at all, where a '5' would mean the answer is crystal clear and defined. Leave emtpy when the question is not applicable or you don't want to answer it, you can skip it without affecting your score. Write your score in the space provided.

After you have responded to all the appropriate statements in each section, compute your average score for that section, using the formula provided, and round to the nearest tenth. Then transfer to the corresponding spoke in the Customer Information Control System Scorecard on the second next page of the Self-Assessment.

Your completed Customer Information Control System Scorecard will give you a clear presentation of which Customer Information Control System areas need attention.

Customer Information Control System Scorecard Example

Example of how the finalized Scorecard can look like:

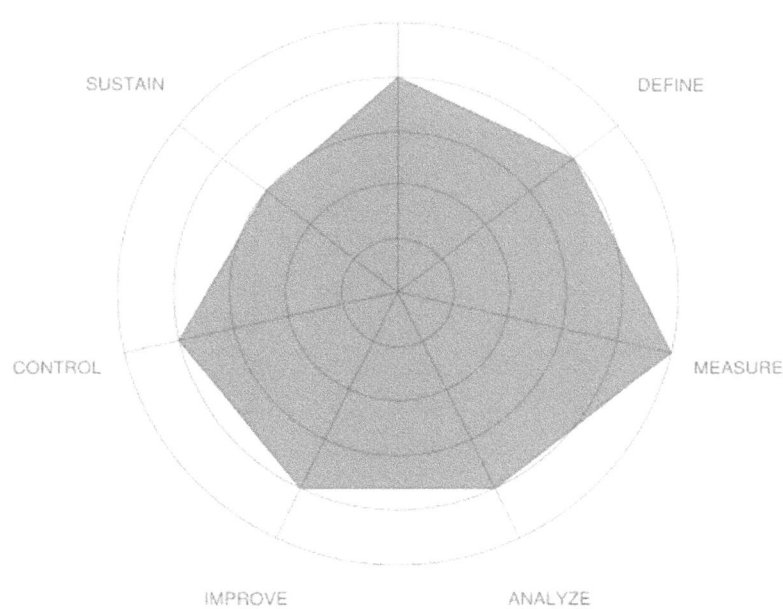

Customer Information Control System Scorecard

Your Scores:

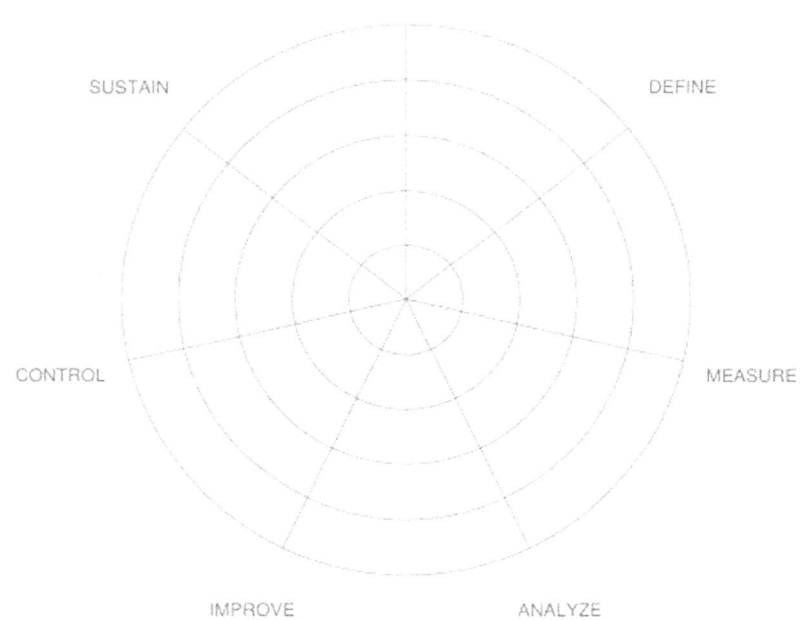

BEGINNING OF THE SELF-ASSESSMENT:

CRITERION #1: RECOGNIZE

INTENT: Be aware of the need for change. Recognize that there is an unfavorable variation, problem or symptom.

In my belief, the answer to this question is clearly defined:

5 Strongly Agree

4 Agree

3 Neutral

2 Disagree

1 Strongly Disagree

1. Does the problem have ethical dimensions?
<--- Score

2. Which issues are too important to ignore?
<--- Score

3. What Customer Information Control System problem should be solved?
<--- Score

4. Who needs budgets?
<--- Score

5. How are the Customer Information Control System's objectives aligned to the group's overall stakeholder strategy?
<--- Score

6. Are your goals realistic? Do you need to redefine your problem? Perhaps the problem has changed or maybe you have reached your goal and need to set a new one?
<--- Score

7. What is the Customer Information Control System problem definition? What do you need to resolve?
<--- Score

8. Consider your own Customer Information Control System project, what types of organizational problems do you think might be causing or affecting your problem, based on the work done so far?
<--- Score

9. Will new equipment/products be required to facilitate Customer Information Control System delivery, for example is new software needed?
<--- Score

10. Will Customer Information Control System deliverables need to be tested and, if so, by whom?
<--- Score

11. What are your needs in relation to Customer

Information Control System skills, labor, equipment, and markets?
<--- Score

12. Are losses recognized in a timely manner?
<--- Score

13. What tools and technologies are needed for a custom Customer Information Control System project?
<--- Score

14. How much are sponsors, customers, partners, stakeholders involved in Customer Information Control System? In other words, what are the risks, if Customer Information Control System does not deliver successfully?
<--- Score

15. Who else hopes to benefit from it?
<--- Score

16. What is the smallest subset of the problem you can usefully solve?
<--- Score

17. What are the expected benefits of Customer Information Control System to the stakeholder?
<--- Score

18. What else needs to be measured?
<--- Score

19. Do you have/need 24-hour access to key personnel?
<--- Score

20. Are there recognized Customer Information Control System problems?
<--- Score

21. Looking at each person individually – does every one have the qualities which are needed to work in this group?
<--- Score

22. Which information does the Customer Information Control System business case need to include?
<--- Score

23. Who defines the rules in relation to any given issue?
<--- Score

24. What needs to be done?
<--- Score

25. How many trainings, in total, are needed?
<--- Score

26. Are employees recognized or rewarded for performance that demonstrates the highest levels of integrity?
<--- Score

27. What is the recognized need?
<--- Score

28. Where do you need to exercise leadership?
<--- Score

29. What are the stakeholder objectives to be

achieved with Customer Information Control System?
<--- Score

30. Are there any revenue recognition issues?
<--- Score

31. What resources or support might you need?
<--- Score

32. Are there Customer Information Control System problems defined?
<--- Score

33. Do you need different information or graphics?
<--- Score

34. Will a response program recognize when a crisis occurs and provide some level of response?
<--- Score

35. Is the need for organizational change recognized?
<--- Score

36. What are the clients issues and concerns?
<--- Score

37. Are you dealing with any of the same issues today as yesterday? What can you do about this?
<--- Score

38. Does Customer Information Control System create potential expectations in other areas that need to be recognized and considered?
<--- Score

39. How do you take a forward-looking perspective

in identifying Customer Information Control System research related to market response and models?
<--- Score

40. Are there any specific expectations or concerns about the Customer Information Control System team, Customer Information Control System itself?
<--- Score

41. What would happen if Customer Information Control System weren't done?
<--- Score

42. What activities does the governance board need to consider?
<--- Score

43. What vendors make products that address the Customer Information Control System needs?
<--- Score

44. Who are your key stakeholders who need to sign off?
<--- Score

45. Do you recognize Customer Information Control System achievements?
<--- Score

46. What are the timeframes required to resolve each of the issues/problems?
<--- Score

47. Is the quality assurance team identified?
<--- Score

48. When a Customer Information Control System manager recognizes a problem, what options are available?
<--- Score

49. How are training requirements identified?
<--- Score

50. How can auditing be a preventative security measure?
<--- Score

51. What Customer Information Control System capabilities do you need?
<--- Score

52. Did you miss any major Customer Information Control System issues?
<--- Score

53. What situation(s) led to this Customer Information Control System Self Assessment?
<--- Score

54. What are the Customer Information Control System resources needed?
<--- Score

55. What should be considered when identifying available resources, constraints, and deadlines?
<--- Score

56. What Customer Information Control System events should you attend?
<--- Score

57. What prevents you from making the changes you know will make you a more effective Customer Information Control System leader?
<--- Score

58. Whom do you really need or want to serve?
<--- Score

59. Think about the people you identified for your Customer Information Control System project and the project responsibilities you would assign to them, what kind of training do you think they would need to perform these responsibilities effectively?
<--- Score

60. Have you identified your Customer Information Control System key performance indicators?
<--- Score

61. Do you know what you need to know about Customer Information Control System?
<--- Score

62. How do you recognize an objection?
<--- Score

63. Are problem definition and motivation clearly presented?
<--- Score

64. What does Customer Information Control System success mean to the stakeholders?
<--- Score

65. What problems are you facing and how do you consider Customer Information Control System will

circumvent those obstacles?
<--- Score

66. What creative shifts do you need to take?
<--- Score

67. How do you identify the kinds of information that you will need?
<--- Score

68. Why the need?
<--- Score

69. How do you identify subcontractor relationships?
<--- Score

70. What extra resources will you need?
<--- Score

71. Would you recognize a threat from the inside?
<--- Score

72. Why is this needed?
<--- Score

73. What do employees need in the short term?
<--- Score

74. What are the minority interests and what amount of minority interests can be recognized?
<--- Score

75. Is it needed?
<--- Score

76. Who needs to know?

<--- Score

77. To what extent does each concerned units management team recognize Customer Information Control System as an effective investment?
<--- Score

78. What Customer Information Control System coordination do you need?
<--- Score

79. How do you assess your Customer Information Control System workforce capability and capacity needs, including skills, competencies, and staffing levels?
<--- Score

80. How does it fit into your organizational needs and tasks?
<--- Score

81. How are you going to measure success?
<--- Score

82. Do you need to avoid or amend any Customer Information Control System activities?
<--- Score

83. Which needs are not included or involved?
<--- Score

84. To what extent would your organization benefit from being recognized as a award recipient?
<--- Score

85. Who should resolve the Customer Information

Control System issues?

<--- Score

86. Will it solve real problems?

<--- Score

87. Are employees recognized for desired behaviors?

<--- Score

88. Who needs to know about Customer Information Control System?

<--- Score

89. Is it clear when you think of the day ahead of you what activities and tasks you need to complete?

<--- Score

90. Are controls defined to recognize and contain problems?

<--- Score

91. What is the problem and/or vulnerability?

<--- Score

92. Does your organization need more Customer Information Control System education?

<--- Score

93. What training and capacity building actions are needed to implement proposed reforms?

<--- Score

94. How do you recognize an Customer Information Control System objection?

<--- Score

95. What information do users need?
<--- Score

96. Where is training needed?
<--- Score

97. What is the extent or complexity of the Customer Information Control System problem?
<--- Score

98. What is the problem or issue?
<--- Score

99. Are there regulatory / compliance issues?
<--- Score

100. As a sponsor, customer or management, how important is it to meet goals, objectives?
<--- Score

101. What needs to stay?
<--- Score

Add up total points for this section:
_ _ _ _ _ = Total points for this section

Divided by: _ _ _ _ _ _ (number of statements answered) = _ _ _ _ _ _
Average score for this section

Transfer your score to the Customer Information Control System Index at the beginning of the Self-Assessment.

CRITERION #2: DEFINE:

INTENT: Formulate the stakeholder problem. Define the problem, needs and objectives.

In my belief, the answer to this question is clearly defined:

5 Strongly Agree

4 Agree

3 Neutral

2 Disagree

1 Strongly Disagree

1. How do you gather Customer Information Control System requirements?
<--- Score

2. Are required metrics defined, what are they?
<--- Score

3. How do you gather requirements?
<--- Score

4. How can the value of Customer Information Control System be defined?
<--- Score

5. Will a Customer Information Control System production readiness review be required?
<--- Score

6. Is the improvement team aware of the different versions of a process: what they think it is vs. what it actually is vs. what it should be vs. what it could be?
<--- Score

7. Is the scope of Customer Information Control System defined?
<--- Score

8. Has the direction changed at all during the course of Customer Information Control System? If so, when did it change and why?
<--- Score

9. Is the Customer Information Control System scope manageable?
<--- Score

10. What Customer Information Control System requirements should be gathered?
<--- Score

11. What are the Customer Information Control System use cases?
<--- Score

12. How do you catch Customer Information Control

System definition inconsistencies?

<--- Score

13. What are the Roles and Responsibilities for each team member and its leadership? Where is this documented?

<--- Score

14. What information do you gather?

<--- Score

15. Are there any constraints known that bear on the ability to perform Customer Information Control System work? How is the team addressing them?

<--- Score

16. Who are the Customer Information Control System improvement team members, including Management Leads and Coaches?

<--- Score

17. How did the Customer Information Control System manager receive input to the development of a Customer Information Control System improvement plan and the estimated completion dates/times of each activity?

<--- Score

18. What is out of scope?

<--- Score

19. Who is gathering information?

<--- Score

20. What is a worst-case scenario for losses?

<--- Score

21. What constraints exist that might impact the team?
<--- Score

22. What are the boundaries of the scope? What is in bounds and what is not? What is the start point? What is the stop point?
<--- Score

23. Is there a clear Customer Information Control System case definition?
<--- Score

24. What is the definition of success?
<--- Score

25. How and when will the baselines be defined?
<--- Score

26. What was the context?
<--- Score

27. Has a high-level 'as is' process map been completed, verified and validated?
<--- Score

28. Is there a Customer Information Control System management charter, including stakeholder case, problem and goal statements, scope, milestones, roles and responsibilities, communication plan?
<--- Score

29. Is special Customer Information Control System user knowledge required?
<--- Score

30. What would be the goal or target for a Customer Information Control System's improvement team?
<--- Score

31. What system do you use for gathering Customer Information Control System information?
<--- Score

32. Is the team adequately staffed with the desired cross-functionality? If not, what additional resources are available to the team?
<--- Score

33. Is there a critical path to deliver Customer Information Control System results?
<--- Score

34. What information should you gather?
<--- Score

35. Has everyone on the team, including the team leaders, been properly trained?
<--- Score

36. Has/have the customer(s) been identified?
<--- Score

37. What are the record-keeping requirements of Customer Information Control System activities?
<--- Score

38. Do you all define Customer Information Control System in the same way?
<--- Score

39. How does the Customer Information Control System manager ensure against scope creep?
<--- Score

40. What is the scope of the Customer Information Control System work?
<--- Score

41. What is the worst case scenario?
<--- Score

42. Do the problem and goal statements meet the SMART criteria (specific, measurable, attainable, relevant, and time-bound)?
<--- Score

43. If substitutes have been appointed, have they been briefed on the Customer Information Control System goals and received regular communications as to the progress to date?
<--- Score

44. How often are the team meetings?
<--- Score

45. What is the scope of Customer Information Control System?
<--- Score

46. How do you gather the stories?
<--- Score

47. What scope do you want your strategy to cover?
<--- Score

48. Have all of the relationships been defined

properly?
<--- Score

49. What customer feedback methods were used to solicit their input?
<--- Score

50. How do you keep key subject matter experts in the loop?
<--- Score

51. Have specific policy objectives been defined?
<--- Score

52. What scope to assess?
<--- Score

53. Is there a completed SIPOC representation, describing the Suppliers, Inputs, Process, Outputs, and Customers?
<--- Score

54. Are approval levels defined for contracts and supplements to contracts?
<--- Score

55. What knowledge or experience is required?
<--- Score

56. Who defines (or who defined) the rules and roles?
<--- Score

57. What is the scope?
<--- Score

58. How do you build the right business case?

<--- Score

59. Has the Customer Information Control System work been fairly and/or equitably divided and delegated among team members who are qualified and capable to perform the work? Has everyone contributed?
<--- Score

60. How have you defined all Customer Information Control System requirements first?
<--- Score

61. What sort of initial information to gather?
<--- Score

62. How do you hand over Customer Information Control System context?
<--- Score

63. Has your scope been defined?
<--- Score

64. Is the current 'as is' process being followed? If not, what are the discrepancies?
<--- Score

65. What is the scope of the Customer Information Control System effort?
<--- Score

66. The political context: who holds power?
<--- Score

67. What is in scope?
<--- Score

68. How will variation in the actual durations of each activity be dealt with to ensure that the expected Customer Information Control System results are met?
<--- Score

69. What specifically is the problem? Where does it occur? When does it occur? What is its extent?
<--- Score

70. Is there a completed, verified, and validated high-level 'as is' (not 'should be' or 'could be') stakeholder process map?
<--- Score

71. Do you have organizational privacy requirements?
<--- Score

72. Have all basic functions of Customer Information Control System been defined?
<--- Score

73. What happens if Customer Information Control System's scope changes?
<--- Score

74. Do you have a Customer Information Control System success story or case study ready to tell and share?
<--- Score

75. Who approved the Customer Information Control System scope?
<--- Score

76. What are the dynamics of the communication plan?

<--- Score

77. Are audit criteria, scope, frequency and methods defined?

<--- Score

78. What are the rough order estimates on cost savings/opportunities that Customer Information Control System brings?

<--- Score

79. What is the context?

<--- Score

80. How would you define the culture at your organization, how susceptible is it to Customer Information Control System changes?

<--- Score

81. What baselines are required to be defined and managed?

<--- Score

82. Is scope creep really all bad news?

<--- Score

83. Is the Customer Information Control System scope complete and appropriately sized?

<--- Score

84. Are task requirements clearly defined?

<--- Score

85. How was the 'as is' process map developed,

reviewed, verified and validated?
<--- Score

86. Are different versions of process maps needed to account for the different types of inputs?
<--- Score

87. How would you define Customer Information Control System leadership?
<--- Score

88. How do you think the partners involved in Customer Information Control System would have defined success?
<--- Score

89. Has anyone else (internal or external to the group) attempted to solve this problem or a similar one before? If so, what knowledge can be leveraged from these previous efforts?
<--- Score

90. What key stakeholder process output measure(s) does Customer Information Control System leverage and how?
<--- Score

91. Is there regularly 100% attendance at the team meetings? If not, have appointed substitutes attended to preserve cross-functionality and full representation?
<--- Score

92. Have the customer needs been translated into specific, measurable requirements? How?
<--- Score

93. When is/was the Customer Information Control System start date?
<--- Score

94. What are the compelling stakeholder reasons for embarking on Customer Information Control System?
<--- Score

95. Are all requirements met?
<--- Score

96. Are the Customer Information Control System requirements complete?
<--- Score

97. What is in the scope and what is not in scope?
<--- Score

98. How will the Customer Information Control System team and the group measure complete success of Customer Information Control System?
<--- Score

99. Are there different segments of customers?
<--- Score

100. What is out-of-scope initially?
<--- Score

101. What are the core elements of the Customer Information Control System business case?
<--- Score

102. What are the requirements for audit information?
<--- Score

103. What are (control) requirements for Customer Information Control System Information?
<--- Score

104. Has a Customer Information Control System requirement not been met?
<--- Score

105. Is it clearly defined in and to your organization what you do?
<--- Score

106. What are the Customer Information Control System tasks and definitions?
<--- Score

107. When are meeting minutes sent out? Who is on the distribution list?
<--- Score

108. When is the estimated completion date?
<--- Score

109. Has the improvement team collected the 'voice of the customer' (obtained feedback – qualitative and quantitative)?
<--- Score

110. Where can you gather more information?
<--- Score

111. How is the team tracking and documenting its work?
<--- Score

112. What is the definition of Customer Information Control System excellence?
<--- Score

113. How do you manage changes in Customer Information Control System requirements?
<--- Score

114. Are accountability and ownership for Customer Information Control System clearly defined?
<--- Score

115. Is Customer Information Control System linked to key stakeholder goals and objectives?
<--- Score

116. Scope of sensitive information?
<--- Score

117. Has a project plan, Gantt chart, or similar been developed/completed?
<--- Score

118. How do you manage unclear Customer Information Control System requirements?
<--- Score

119. In what way can you redefine the criteria of choice clients have in your category in your favor?
<--- Score

120. Is data collected and displayed to better understand customer(s) critical needs and requirements.
<--- Score

121. What critical content must be communicated –
who, what, when, where, and how?
<--- Score

122. What gets examined?
<--- Score

**123. What sources do you use to gather
information for a Customer Information Control
System study?**
<--- Score

**124. How are consistent Customer Information
Control System definitions important?**
<--- Score

**125. Is there any additional Customer Information
Control System definition of success?**
<--- Score

126. Is Customer Information Control System
required?
<--- Score

127. Is the team equipped with available and reliable
resources?
<--- Score

128. Are customer(s) identified and segmented
according to their different needs and requirements?
<--- Score

129. Is Customer Information Control System currently
on schedule according to the plan?
<--- Score

130. Does the scope remain the same?
<--- Score

131. Has a team charter been developed and communicated?
<--- Score

132. Will team members regularly document their Customer Information Control System work?
<--- Score

133. Does the team have regular meetings?
<--- Score

134. What are the tasks and definitions?
<--- Score

135. How do you manage scope?
<--- Score

Add up total points for this section:
_____ = Total points for this section

Divided by: _____ (number of statements answered) = _____
Average score for this section

Transfer your score to the Customer Information Control System Index at the beginning of the Self-Assessment.

CRITERION #3: MEASURE:

In my belief, the answer to this question is clearly defined:

5 Strongly Agree

4 Agree

3 Neutral

2 Disagree

1 Strongly Disagree

1. How do you verify if Customer Information Control System is built right?
<--- Score

2. How do you verify your resources?
<--- Score

3. Will Customer Information Control System have an impact on current business continuity, disaster

recovery processes and/or infrastructure?
<--- Score

4. What would it cost to replace your technology?
<--- Score

5. Why a Customer Information Control System focus?
<--- Score

6. What are your customers expectations and measures?
<--- Score

7. Are indirect costs charged to the Customer Information Control System program?
<--- Score

8. Who pays the cost?
<--- Score

9. Among the Customer Information Control System product and service cost to be estimated, which is considered hardest to estimate?
<--- Score

10. What is measured? Why?
<--- Score

11. What are the costs?
<--- Score

12. How do you measure success?
<--- Score

13. Have you made assumptions about the shape of

the future, particularly its impact on your customers
and competitors?
<--- Score

14. Is the scope of Customer Information Control
System cost analysis cost-effective?
<--- Score

15. How can you reduce the costs of obtaining inputs?
<--- Score

**16. How do you focus on what is right -not who is
right?**
<--- Score

17. When should you bother with diagrams?
<--- Score

18. What does verifying compliance entail?
<--- Score

19. How are you verifying it?
<--- Score

20. What potential environmental factors impact the
Customer Information Control System effort?
<--- Score

21. How can you measure the performance?
<--- Score

22. How do you measure efficient delivery of
Customer Information Control System services?
<--- Score

23. How do you measure variability?

<--- Score

24. What is the Customer Information Control System business impact?
<--- Score

25. What can be used to verify compliance?
<--- Score

26. How will your organization measure success?
<--- Score

27. What are your operating costs?
<--- Score

28. Have design-to-cost goals been established?
<--- Score

29. Which Customer Information Control System impacts are significant?
<--- Score

30. Is it possible to estimate the impact of unanticipated complexity such as wrong or failed assumptions, feedback, etcetera on proposed reforms?
<--- Score

31. What is your decision requirements diagram?
<--- Score

32. How do you prevent mis-estimating cost?
<--- Score

33. How will effects be measured?
<--- Score

34. How do you verify Customer Information Control System completeness and accuracy?

<--- Score

35. Does a Customer Information Control System quantification method exist?

<--- Score

36. What causes extra work or rework?

<--- Score

37. When a disaster occurs, who gets priority?

<--- Score

38. What relevant entities could be measured?

<--- Score

39. What is your Customer Information Control System quality cost segregation study?

<--- Score

40. Are missed Customer Information Control System opportunities costing your organization money?

<--- Score

41. What is the root cause(s) of the problem?

<--- Score

42. How does cost-to-serve analysis help?

<--- Score

43. What are you verifying?

<--- Score

44. What are the Customer Information Control

System investment costs?
<--- Score

45. Do you have an issue in getting priority?
<--- Score

46. What drives O&M cost?
<--- Score

47. What are hidden Customer Information Control System quality costs?
<--- Score

48. How will costs be allocated?
<--- Score

49. How can a Customer Information Control System test verify your ideas or assumptions?
<--- Score

50. Which costs should be taken into account?
<--- Score

51. How frequently do you verify your Customer Information Control System strategy?
<--- Score

52. What are the costs and benefits?
<--- Score

53. How can you reduce costs?
<--- Score

54. How do you verify and develop ideas and innovations?
<--- Score

55. How will success or failure be measured?
<--- Score

56. How do you quantify and qualify impacts?
<--- Score

57. Are the Customer Information Control System benefits worth its costs?
<--- Score

58. What harm might be caused?
<--- Score

59. Does the Customer Information Control System task fit the client's priorities?
<--- Score

60. Are you aware of what could cause a problem?
<--- Score

61. How will you measure success?
<--- Score

62. What is the cause of any Customer Information Control System gaps?
<--- Score

63. Are actual costs in line with budgeted costs?
<--- Score

64. At what cost?
<--- Score

65. Has a cost center been established?
<--- Score

66. What disadvantage does this cause for the user?
<--- Score

67. What does losing customers cost your organization?
<--- Score

68. Is there an opportunity to verify requirements?
<--- Score

69. Which measures and indicators matter?
<--- Score

70. What causes innovation to fail or succeed in your organization?
<--- Score

71. Are supply costs steady or fluctuating?
<--- Score

72. What are the strategic priorities for this year?
<--- Score

73. Do you aggressively reward and promote the people who have the biggest impact on creating excellent Customer Information Control System services/products?
<--- Score

74. Why do the measurements/indicators matter?
<--- Score

75. Did you tackle the cause or the symptom?
<--- Score

76. How will measures be used to manage and adapt?
<--- Score

77. How is progress measured?
<--- Score

78. Do you have any cost Customer Information Control System limitation requirements?
<--- Score

79. What are the costs of reform?
<--- Score

80. Are there measurements based on task performance?
<--- Score

81. How to cause the change?
<--- Score

82. Are you taking your company in the direction of better and revenue or cheaper and cost?
<--- Score

83. Do you verify that corrective actions were taken?
<--- Score

84. How do you measure lifecycle phases?
<--- Score

85. How do your measurements capture actionable Customer Information Control System information for use in exceeding your customers expectations and securing your customers engagement?
<--- Score

86. How sensitive must the Customer Information Control System strategy be to cost?
<--- Score

87. What are the operational costs after Customer Information Control System deployment?
<--- Score

88. How long to keep data and how to manage retention costs?
<--- Score

89. How do you verify the Customer Information Control System requirements quality?
<--- Score

90. What are the current costs of the Customer Information Control System process?
<--- Score

91. Are the units of measure consistent?
<--- Score

92. What does your operating model cost?
<--- Score

93. How is performance measured?
<--- Score

94. Are Customer Information Control System vulnerabilities categorized and prioritized?
<--- Score

95. How can you manage cost down?
<--- Score

96. Is a follow-up focused external Customer Information Control System review required?
<--- Score

97. What tests verify requirements?
<--- Score

98. Where is it measured?
<--- Score

99. What are allowable costs?
<--- Score

100. Why do you expend time and effort to implement measurement, for whom?
<--- Score

101. What could cause delays in the schedule?
<--- Score

102. Was a business case (cost/benefit) developed?
<--- Score

103. Where is the cost?
<--- Score

104. How can you measure Customer Information Control System in a systematic way?
<--- Score

105. Is the cost worth the Customer Information Control System effort ?
<--- Score

106. How are measurements made?
<--- Score

107. How is the value delivered by Customer Information Control System being measured?

<--- Score

108. What happens if cost savings do not materialize?

<--- Score

109. What is your cost benefit analysis?

<--- Score

110. What are your key Customer Information Control System organizational performance measures, including key short and longer-term financial measures?

<--- Score

111. What are the uncertainties surrounding estimates of impact?

<--- Score

112. What could cause you to change course?

<--- Score

113. What measurements are possible, practicable and meaningful?

<--- Score

114. What is the cost of rework?

<--- Score

115. How will you measure your Customer Information Control System effectiveness?

<--- Score

116. What causes investor action?

<--- Score

117. What is the total fixed cost?
<--- Score

118. Was a life-cycle cost analysis performed?
<--- Score

119. How do you control the overall costs of your work processes?
<--- Score

120. Is the solution cost-effective?
<--- Score

121. What is an unallowable cost?
<--- Score

122. Who should receive measurement reports?
<--- Score

123. How much does it cost?
<--- Score

124. How frequently do you track Customer Information Control System measures?
<--- Score

125. What does a Test Case verify?
<--- Score

126. What do you measure and why?
<--- Score

127. How will the Customer Information Control System data be analyzed?

<--- Score

128. What is the total cost related to deploying Customer Information Control System, including any consulting or professional services?
<--- Score

129. How do you verify and validate the Customer Information Control System data?
<--- Score

130. How do you stay flexible and focused to recognize larger Customer Information Control System results?
<--- Score

131. The approach of traditional Customer Information Control System works for detail complexity but is focused on a systematic approach rather than an understanding of the nature of systems themselves, what approach will permit your organization to deal with the kind of unpredictable emergent behaviors that dynamic complexity can introduce?
<--- Score

132. What are predictive Customer Information Control System analytics?
<--- Score

133. What methods are feasible and acceptable to estimate the impact of reforms?
<--- Score

134. What do people want to verify?
<--- Score

135. Are the measurements objective?
<--- Score

136. How do you verify performance?
<--- Score

137. Do the benefits outweigh the costs?
<--- Score

138. Are there competing Customer Information Control System priorities?
<--- Score

139. How do you aggregate measures across priorities?
<--- Score

140. Are there any easy-to-implement alternatives to Customer Information Control System? Sometimes other solutions are available that do not require the cost implications of a full-blown project?
<--- Score

141. Have you included everything in your Customer Information Control System cost models?
<--- Score

Add up total points for this section:
_ _ _ _ _ = Total points for this section

Divided by: _ _ _ _ _ _ (number of statements answered) = _ _ _ _ _ _
Average score for this section

Transfer your score to the Customer

Information Control System Index at the beginning of the Self-Assessment.

CRITERION #4: ANALYZE:

INTENT: Analyze causes, assumptions and hypotheses.

In my belief, the answer to this question is clearly defined:

5 Strongly Agree

4 Agree

3 Neutral

2 Disagree

1 Strongly Disagree

1. Were Pareto charts (or similar) used to portray the 'heavy hitters' (or key sources of variation)?
<--- Score

2. Is data and process analysis, root cause analysis and quantifying the gap/opportunity in place?
<--- Score

3. What are your best practices for minimizing Customer Information Control System project

risk, while demonstrating incremental value and quick wins throughout the Customer Information Control System project lifecycle?

<--- Score

4. What are the disruptive Customer Information Control System technologies that enable your organization to radically change your business processes?

<--- Score

5. How was the detailed process map generated, verified, and validated?

<--- Score

6. What Customer Information Control System data should be managed?

<--- Score

7. Where can you get qualified talent today?

<--- Score

8. Are gaps between current performance and the goal performance identified?

<--- Score

9. Think about some of the processes you undertake within your organization, which do you own?

<--- Score

10. What Customer Information Control System data do you gather or use now?

<--- Score

11. When should a process be art not science?

<--- Score

12. What quality tools were used to get through the analyze phase?
<--- Score

13. Is the required Customer Information Control System data gathered?
<--- Score

14. Who is involved in the management review process?
<--- Score

15. What is the oversight process?
<--- Score

16. How do mission and objectives affect the Customer Information Control System processes of your organization?
<--- Score

17. Who gets your output?
<--- Score

18. What are the best opportunities for value improvement?
<--- Score

19. Are you missing Customer Information Control System opportunities?
<--- Score

20. Should you invest in industry-recognized qualifications?
<--- Score

21. What are the Customer Information Control System design outputs?
<--- Score

22. Who owns what data?
<--- Score

23. Is there a strict change management process?
<--- Score

24. A compounding model resolution with available relevant data can often provide insight towards a solution methodology; which Customer Information Control System models, tools and techniques are necessary?
<--- Score

25. Identify an operational issue in your organization, for example, could a particular task be done more quickly or more efficiently by Customer Information Control System?
<--- Score

26. What do you need to qualify?
<--- Score

27. Was a cause-and-effect diagram used to explore the different types of causes (or sources of variation)?
<--- Score

28. What Customer Information Control System metrics are outputs of the process?
<--- Score

29. What were the financial benefits resulting from any 'ground fruit or low-hanging fruit' (quick fixes)?

<--- Score

30. How do you promote understanding that opportunity for improvement is not criticism of the status quo, or the people who created the status quo?
<--- Score

31. What are your key performance measures or indicators and in-process measures for the control and improvement of your Customer Information Control System processes?
<--- Score

32. What systems/processes must you excel at?
<--- Score

33. What is your organizations system for selecting qualified vendors?
<--- Score

34. How do you define collaboration and team output?
<--- Score

35. How difficult is it to qualify what Customer Information Control System ROI is?
<--- Score

36. What information qualified as important?
<--- Score

37. What resources go in to get the desired output?
<--- Score

38. Do your employees have the opportunity to do what they do best everyday?

<--- Score

39. What training and qualifications will you need?
<--- Score

40. Was a detailed process map created to amplify critical steps of the 'as is' stakeholder process?
<--- Score

41. Can you add value to the current Customer Information Control System decision-making process (largely qualitative) by incorporating uncertainty modeling (more quantitative)?
<--- Score

42. How do you identify specific Customer Information Control System investment opportunities and emerging trends?
<--- Score

43. What tools were used to generate the list of possible causes?
<--- Score

44. What data do you need to collect?
<--- Score

45. How do your work systems and key work processes relate to and capitalize on your core competencies?
<--- Score

46. Is the Customer Information Control System process severely broken such that a re-design is necessary?
<--- Score

47. What is the complexity of the output produced?
<--- Score

48. Were any designed experiments used to generate additional insight into the data analysis?
<--- Score

49. How do you ensure that the Customer Information Control System opportunity is realistic?
<--- Score

50. How has the Customer Information Control System data been gathered?
<--- Score

51. Do your contracts/agreements contain data security obligations?
<--- Score

52. What will drive Customer Information Control System change?
<--- Score

53. Has an output goal been set?
<--- Score

54. How is data used for program management and improvement?
<--- Score

55. What are the personnel training and qualifications required?
<--- Score

56. What are the Customer Information Control

System business drivers?

<--- Score

57. How do you implement and manage your work processes to ensure that they meet design requirements?

<--- Score

58. How will the change process be managed?

<--- Score

59. Where is the data coming from to measure compliance?

<--- Score

60. Do staff qualifications match your project?

<--- Score

61. Do you understand your management processes today?

<--- Score

62. Which Customer Information Control System data should be retained?

<--- Score

63. What process improvements will be needed?

<--- Score

64. What does the data say about the performance of the stakeholder process?

<--- Score

65. What other organizational variables, such as reward systems or communication systems, affect the performance of this Customer Information Control

System process?

<--- Score

66. How do you use Customer Information Control System data and information to support organizational decision making and innovation?

<--- Score

67. Think about the functions involved in your Customer Information Control System project, what processes flow from these functions?

<--- Score

68. How many input/output points does it require?

<--- Score

69. What are evaluation criteria for the output?

<--- Score

70. Are Customer Information Control System changes recognized early enough to be approved through the regular process?

<--- Score

71. How is the Customer Information Control System Value Stream Mapping managed?

<--- Score

72. How will the Customer Information Control System data be captured?

<--- Score

73. Are all team members qualified for all tasks?

<--- Score

74. What conclusions were drawn from the team's

data collection and analysis? How did the team reach these conclusions?

<--- Score

75. Are your outputs consistent?

<--- Score

76. What successful thing are you doing today that may be blinding you to new growth opportunities?

<--- Score

77. Are all staff in core Customer Information Control System subjects Highly Qualified?

<--- Score

78. What other jobs or tasks affect the performance of the steps in the Customer Information Control System process?

<--- Score

79. Where is Customer Information Control System data gathered?

<--- Score

80. What are your outputs?

<--- Score

81. An organizationally feasible system request is one that considers the mission, goals and objectives of the organization, key questions are: is the Customer Information Control System solution request practical and will it solve a problem or take advantage of an opportunity to achieve company goals?

<--- Score

82. Have you defined which data is gathered how?

<--- Score

83. How are outputs preserved and protected?
<--- Score

84. How do you measure the operational performance of your key work systems and processes, including productivity, cycle time, and other appropriate measures of process effectiveness, efficiency, and innovation?
<--- Score

85. How often will data be collected for measures?
<--- Score

86. What, related to, Customer Information Control System processes does your organization outsource?
<--- Score

87. What are your Customer Information Control System processes?
<--- Score

88. Is the final output clearly identified?
<--- Score

89. What is the cost of poor quality as supported by the team's analysis?
<--- Score

90. Is the performance gap determined?
<--- Score

91. Is there any way to speed up the process?
<--- Score

92. Did any value-added analysis or 'lean thinking' take place to identify some of the gaps shown on the 'as is' process map?
<--- Score

93. What is your organizations process which leads to recognition of value generation?
<--- Score

94. Were there any improvement opportunities identified from the process analysis?
<--- Score

95. Do you have the authority to produce the output?
<--- Score

96. Has data output been validated?
<--- Score

97. What is the output?
<--- Score

98. What tools were used to narrow the list of possible causes?
<--- Score

99. Who is involved with workflow mapping?
<--- Score

100. What methods do you use to gather Customer Information Control System data?
<--- Score

101. How is the way you as the leader think and process information affecting your organizational culture?

<--- Score

102. What types of data do your Customer Information Control System indicators require?
<--- Score

103. What data is gathered?
<--- Score

104. Record-keeping requirements flow from the records needed as inputs, outputs, controls and for transformation of a Customer Information Control System process, are the records needed as inputs to the Customer Information Control System process available?
<--- Score

105. Do quality systems drive continuous improvement?
<--- Score

106. What qualifications are necessary?
<--- Score

107. How does the organization define, manage, and improve its Customer Information Control System processes?
<--- Score

108. What kind of crime could a potential new hire have committed that would not only not disqualify him/her from being hired by your organization, but would actually indicate that he/she might be a particularly good fit?
<--- Score

109. Who will facilitate the team and process?
<--- Score

110. Did any additional data need to be collected?
<--- Score

111. Is the suppliers process defined and controlled?
<--- Score

112. What did the team gain from developing a sub-process map?
<--- Score

113. What are your current levels and trends in key measures or indicators of Customer Information Control System product and process performance that are important to and directly serve your customers? How do these results compare with the performance of your competitors and other organizations with similar offerings?
<--- Score

114. What internal processes need improvement?
<--- Score

115. What qualifications do Customer Information Control System leaders need?
<--- Score

116. Do several people in different organizational units assist with the Customer Information Control System process?
<--- Score

117. What qualifies as competition?

<--- Score

118. Have the problem and goal statements been updated to reflect the additional knowledge gained from the analyze phase?
<--- Score

119. Do your leaders quickly bounce back from setbacks?
<--- Score

120. What qualifications are needed?
<--- Score

121. What were the crucial 'moments of truth' on the process map?
<--- Score

122. What are the revised rough estimates of the financial savings/opportunity for Customer Information Control System improvements?
<--- Score

123. Have any additional benefits been identified that will result from closing all or most of the gaps?
<--- Score

124. Is pre-qualification of suppliers carried out?
<--- Score

125. How will corresponding data be collected?
<--- Score

126. How can risk management be tied procedurally to process elements?
<--- Score

127. What is the Customer Information Control System Driver?
<--- Score

128. Is there an established change management process?
<--- Score

129. What output to create?
<--- Score

130. Who qualifies to gain access to data?
<--- Score

131. Who will gather what data?
<--- Score

132. Is the gap/opportunity displayed and communicated in financial terms?
<--- Score

Add up total points for this section:
_ _ _ _ _ = Total points for this section

Divided by: _ _ _ _ _ _ (number of statements answered) = _ _ _ _ _ _
Average score for this section

Transfer your score to the Customer Information Control System Index at the beginning of the Self-Assessment.

CRITERION #5: IMPROVE:

INTENT: Develop a practical solution. Innovate, establish and test the solution and to measure the results.

In my belief, the answer to this question is clearly defined:

5 Strongly Agree

4 Agree

3 Neutral

2 Disagree

1 Strongly Disagree

1. Is there any other Customer Information Control System solution?
<--- Score

2. What are the implications of the one critical Customer Information Control System decision 10 minutes, 10 months, and 10 years from now?
<--- Score

3. How can skill-level changes improve Customer Information Control System?
<--- Score

4. How do you measure risk?
<--- Score

5. Is supporting Customer Information Control System documentation required?
<--- Score

6. What do you want to improve?
<--- Score

7. How do you keep improving Customer Information Control System?
<--- Score

8. For estimation problems, how do you develop an estimation statement?
<--- Score

9. Are you assessing Customer Information Control System and risk?
<--- Score

10. What needs improvement? Why?
<--- Score

11. How can you better manage risk?
<--- Score

12. Who makes the Customer Information Control System decisions in your organization?
<--- Score

13. Is the Customer Information Control System risk managed?
<--- Score

14. Would you develop a Customer Information Control System Communication Strategy?
<--- Score

15. What criteria will you use to assess your Customer Information Control System risks?
<--- Score

16. How are Customer Information Control System risks managed?
<--- Score

17. What tools were used to tap into the creativity and encourage 'outside the box' thinking?
<--- Score

18. Who controls the risk?
<--- Score

19. Do those selected for the Customer Information Control System team have a good general understanding of what Customer Information Control System is all about?
<--- Score

20. What is Customer Information Control System's impact on utilizing the best solution(s)?
<--- Score

21. What assumptions are made about the solution and approach?
<--- Score

22. What attendant changes will need to be made to ensure that the solution is successful?
<--- Score

23. Where do the Customer Information Control System decisions reside?
<--- Score

24. Can you integrate quality management and risk management?
<--- Score

25. When you map the key players in your own work and the types/domains of relationships with them, which relationships do you find easy and which challenging, and why?
<--- Score

26. Customer Information Control System risk decisions: whose call Is It?
<--- Score

27. Who will be using the results of the measurement activities?
<--- Score

28. How do you manage Customer Information Control System risk?
<--- Score

29. Who will be responsible for documenting the Customer Information Control System requirements in detail?
<--- Score

30. What are the affordable Customer Information Control System risks?
<--- Score

31. Do you need to do a usability evaluation?
<--- Score

32. What are your current levels and trends in key measures or indicators of workforce and leader development?
<--- Score

33. Can you identify any significant risks or exposures to Customer Information Control System third- parties (vendors, service providers, alliance partners etc) that concern you?
<--- Score

34. How do you define the solutions' scope?
<--- Score

35. Is the Customer Information Control System documentation thorough?
<--- Score

36. Who are the people involved in developing and implementing Customer Information Control System?
<--- Score

37. What communications are necessary to support the implementation of the solution?
<--- Score

38. What tools do you use once you have decided on a Customer Information Control System strategy and more importantly how do you choose?

<--- Score

39. Is there a cost/benefit analysis of optimal solution(s)?
<--- Score

40. Are the most efficient solutions problem-specific?
<--- Score

41. Will the controls trigger any other risks?
<--- Score

42. How will you know that you have improved?
<--- Score

43. What area needs the greatest improvement?
<--- Score

44. Who should make the Customer Information Control System decisions?
<--- Score

45. Where do you need Customer Information Control System improvement?
<--- Score

46. How are policy decisions made and where?
<--- Score

47. What is the risk?
<--- Score

48. How do you improve productivity?
<--- Score

49. Can the solution be designed and

implemented within an acceptable time period?
<--- Score

50. What are the expected Customer Information Control System results?
<--- Score

51. Do you combine technical expertise with business knowledge and Customer Information Control System Key topics include lifecycles, development approaches, requirements and how to make a business case?
<--- Score

52. Is any Customer Information Control System documentation required?
<--- Score

53. What tools were used to evaluate the potential solutions?
<--- Score

54. Are the key business and technology risks being managed?
<--- Score

55. What resources are required for the improvement efforts?
<--- Score

56. How do you measure improved Customer Information Control System service perception, and satisfaction?
<--- Score

57. How do you improve Customer Information

Control System service perception, and satisfaction?
<--- Score

58. How do you link measurement and risk?
<--- Score

59. How can you improve Customer Information Control System?
<--- Score

60. How will you measure the results?
<--- Score

61. Are the risks fully understood, reasonable and manageable?
<--- Score

62. What error proofing will be done to address some of the discrepancies observed in the 'as is' process?
<--- Score

63. What current systems have to be understood and/ or changed?
<--- Score

64. How risky is your organization?
<--- Score

65. At what point will vulnerability assessments be performed once Customer Information Control System is put into production (e.g., ongoing Risk Management after implementation)?
<--- Score

66. Who are the Customer Information Control System decision-makers?

<--- Score

67. What actually has to improve and by how much?
<--- Score

68. Is the optimal solution selected based on testing and analysis?
<--- Score

69. How is continuous improvement applied to risk management?
<--- Score

70. Have you identified breakpoints and/or risk tolerances that will trigger broad consideration of a potential need for intervention or modification of strategy?
<--- Score

71. Are decisions made in a timely manner?
<--- Score

72. Who will be responsible for making the decisions to include or exclude requested changes once Customer Information Control System is underway?
<--- Score

73. How will you know that a change is an improvement?
<--- Score

74. Who are the key stakeholders for the Customer Information Control System evaluation?
<--- Score

75. Was a Customer Information Control System

charter developed?
<--- Score

76. Why improve in the first place?
<--- Score

77. If you could go back in time five years, what decision would you make differently? What is your best guess as to what decision you're making today you might regret five years from now?
<--- Score

78. Is the measure of success for Customer Information Control System understandable to a variety of people?
<--- Score

79. What went well, what should change, what can improve?
<--- Score

80. Risk Identification: What are the possible risk events your organization faces in relation to Customer Information Control System?
<--- Score

81. Do vendor agreements bring new compliance risk ?
<--- Score

82. Are events managed to resolution?
<--- Score

83. What can you do to improve?
<--- Score

84. What are the concrete Customer Information Control System results?
<--- Score

85. What risks do you need to manage?
<--- Score

86. Is the Customer Information Control System solution sustainable?
<--- Score

87. Explorations of the frontiers of Customer Information Control System will help you build influence, improve Customer Information Control System, optimize decision making, and sustain change, what is your approach?
<--- Score

88. Who manages Customer Information Control System risk?
<--- Score

89. What is the implementation plan?
<--- Score

90. Is the solution technically practical?
<--- Score

91. How do you decide how much to remunerate an employee?
<--- Score

92. What to do with the results or outcomes of measurements?
<--- Score

93. Who do you report Customer Information Control System results to?
<--- Score

94. Do you cover the five essential competencies: Communication, Collaboration,Innovation, Adaptability, and Leadership that improve an organizations ability to leverage the new Customer Information Control System in a volatile global economy?
<--- Score

95. Was a pilot designed for the proposed solution(s)?
<--- Score

96. What is the Customer Information Control System's sustainability risk?
<--- Score

97. What is the team's contingency plan for potential problems occurring in implementation?
<--- Score

98. For decision problems, how do you develop a decision statement?
<--- Score

99. Does a good decision guarantee a good outcome?
<--- Score

100. How do the Customer Information Control System results compare with the performance of your competitors and other organizations with similar offerings?
<--- Score

101. How scalable is your Customer Information Control System solution?
<--- Score

102. What lessons, if any, from a pilot were incorporated into the design of the full-scale solution?
<--- Score

103. Were any criteria developed to assist the team in testing and evaluating potential solutions?
<--- Score

104. What Customer Information Control System improvements can be made?
<--- Score

105. To what extent does management recognize Customer Information Control System as a tool to increase the results?
<--- Score

106. What practices helps your organization to develop its capacity to recognize patterns?
<--- Score

107. How do you manage and improve your Customer Information Control System work systems to deliver customer value and achieve organizational success and sustainability?
<--- Score

108. What strategies for Customer Information Control System improvement are successful?
<--- Score

109. Is there a small-scale pilot for proposed improvement(s)? What conclusions were drawn from the outcomes of a pilot?
<--- Score

110. Are risk management tasks balanced centrally and locally?
<--- Score

111. How will you recognize and celebrate results?
<--- Score

112. What is the magnitude of the improvements?
<--- Score

113. What were the underlying assumptions on the cost-benefit analysis?
<--- Score

114. In the past few months, what is the smallest change you have made that has had the biggest positive result? What was it about that small change that produced the large return?
<--- Score

115. Have you achieved Customer Information Control System improvements?
<--- Score

116. Which Customer Information Control System solution is appropriate?
<--- Score

117. How do you mitigate Customer Information Control System risk?
<--- Score

118. Risk factors: what are the characteristics of Customer Information Control System that make it risky?
<--- Score

119. How can the phases of Customer Information Control System development be identified?
<--- Score

120. What does the 'should be' process map/design look like?
<--- Score

121. Is the scope clearly documented?
<--- Score

122. Does the goal represent a desired result that can be measured?
<--- Score

123. Is risk periodically assessed?
<--- Score

124. How do you improve your likelihood of success ?
<--- Score

125. How does the team improve its work?
<--- Score

126. What improvements have been achieved?
<--- Score

127. What should a proof of concept or pilot accomplish?

<--- Score

128. What tools were most useful during the improve phase?
<--- Score

129. Is Customer Information Control System documentation maintained?
<--- Score

130. Who controls key decisions that will be made?
<--- Score

131. How can you improve performance?
<--- Score

132. Who are the Customer Information Control System decision makers?
<--- Score

133. How does your organization evaluate strategic Customer Information Control System success?
<--- Score

134. How do you measure progress and evaluate training effectiveness?
<--- Score

135. Do you have the optimal project management team structure?
<--- Score

136. Which of the recognised risks out of all risks can be most likely transferred?
<--- Score

137. Risk events: what are the things that could go wrong?

<--- Score

Add up total points for this section:
_____ = Total points for this section

Divided by: _____ (number of
statements answered) = _____
Average score for this section

Transfer your score to the Customer
Information Control System Index at the
beginning of the Self-Assessment.

CRITERION #6: CONTROL:

INTENT: Implement the practical
solution. Maintain the performance and
correct possible complications.

In my belief, the answer to this
question is clearly defined:

5 Strongly Agree

4 Agree

3 Neutral

2 Disagree

1 Strongly Disagree

1. Has the improved process and its steps been standardized?
<--- Score

2. What are customers monitoring?
<--- Score

3. Can support from partners be adjusted?
<--- Score

4. What Customer Information Control System standards are applicable?

<--- Score

5. What adjustments to the strategies are needed?

<--- Score

6. Is there a documented and implemented monitoring plan?

<--- Score

7. What are the known security controls?

<--- Score

8. Is there a standardized process?

<--- Score

9. Can you adapt and adjust to changing Customer Information Control System situations?

<--- Score

10. Is there documentation that will support the successful operation of the improvement?

<--- Score

11. What do you stand for--and what are you against?

<--- Score

12. What can you control?

<--- Score

13. Does a troubleshooting guide exist or is it needed?

<--- Score

14. Is a response plan established and deployed?
<--- Score

15. How is Customer Information Control System project cost planned, managed, monitored?
<--- Score

16. How do you establish and deploy modified action plans if circumstances require a shift in plans and rapid execution of new plans?
<--- Score

17. How will new or emerging customer needs/ requirements be checked/communicated to orient the process toward meeting the new specifications and continually reducing variation?
<--- Score

18. In the case of a Customer Information Control System project, the criteria for the audit derive from implementation objectives, an audit of a Customer Information Control System project involves assessing whether the recommendations outlined for implementation have been met, can you track that any Customer Information Control System project is implemented as planned, and is it working?
<--- Score

19. Are operating procedures consistent?
<--- Score

20. How is change control managed?
<--- Score

21. How likely is the current Customer Information Control System plan to come in on schedule or on

budget?
<--- Score

22. Will existing staff require re-training, for example, to learn new business processes?
<--- Score

23. What are you attempting to measure/monitor?
<--- Score

24. Is knowledge gained on process shared and institutionalized?
<--- Score

25. Are the Customer Information Control System standards challenging?
<--- Score

26. Do you monitor the effectiveness of your Customer Information Control System activities?
<--- Score

27. Does the Customer Information Control System performance meet the customer's requirements?
<--- Score

28. Are controls in place and consistently applied?
<--- Score

29. What is your plan to assess your security risks?
<--- Score

30. Are documented procedures clear and easy to follow for the operators?
<--- Score

31. What is the recommended frequency of auditing?
<--- Score

32. What other areas of the group might benefit from the Customer Information Control System team's improvements, knowledge, and learning?
<--- Score

33. Are the planned controls in place?
<--- Score

34. How do you encourage people to take control and responsibility?
<--- Score

35. Will your goals reflect your program budget?
<--- Score

36. Is new knowledge gained imbedded in the response plan?
<--- Score

37. Are suggested corrective/restorative actions indicated on the response plan for known causes to problems that might surface?
<--- Score

38. Who is going to spread your message?
<--- Score

39. What do your reports reflect?
<--- Score

40. Is there an action plan in case of emergencies?
<--- Score

41. Is there a transfer of ownership and knowledge to process owner and process team tasked with the responsibilities.
<--- Score

42. Is there a recommended audit plan for routine surveillance inspections of Customer Information Control System's gains?
<--- Score

43. Where do ideas that reach policy makers and planners as proposals for Customer Information Control System strengthening and reform actually originate?
<--- Score

44. How widespread is its use?
<--- Score

45. How do you plan for the cost of succession?
<--- Score

46. How will the process owner verify improvement in present and future sigma levels, process capabilities?
<--- Score

47. What key inputs and outputs are being measured on an ongoing basis?
<--- Score

48. Is there a control plan in place for sustaining improvements (short and long-term)?
<--- Score

49. How will the process owner and team be able to hold the gains?

<--- Score

50. How do controls support value?
<--- Score

51. What are the key elements of your Customer Information Control System performance improvement system, including your evaluation, organizational learning, and innovation processes?
<--- Score

52. How do you plan on providing proper recognition and disclosure of supporting companies?
<--- Score

53. Are new process steps, standards, and documentation ingrained into normal operations?
<--- Score

54. Does the response plan contain a definite closed loop continual improvement scheme (e.g., plan-do-check-act)?
<--- Score

55. Are you measuring, monitoring and predicting Customer Information Control System activities to optimize operations and profitability, and enhancing outcomes?
<--- Score

56. Does job training on the documented procedures need to be part of the process team's education and training?
<--- Score

57. How do you monitor usage and cost?

<--- Score

58. Will the team be available to assist members in planning investigations?
<--- Score

59. Do you monitor the Customer Information Control System decisions made and fine tune them as they evolve?
<--- Score

60. Will any special training be provided for results interpretation?
<--- Score

61. Act/Adjust: What Do you Need to Do Differently?
<--- Score

62. You may have created your quality measures at a time when you lacked resources, technology wasn't up to the required standard, or low service levels were the industry norm. Have those circumstances changed?
<--- Score

63. Is reporting being used or needed?
<--- Score

64. What should you measure to verify efficiency gains?
<--- Score

65. What do you measure to verify effectiveness gains?
<--- Score

66. How do you select, collect, align, and integrate Customer Information Control System data and information for tracking daily operations and overall organizational performance, including progress relative to strategic objectives and action plans?
<--- Score

67. Do the viable solutions scale to future needs?
<--- Score

68. What are the performance and scale of the Customer Information Control System tools?
<--- Score

69. What is the control/monitoring plan?
<--- Score

70. Is a response plan in place for when the input, process, or output measures indicate an 'out-of-control' condition?
<--- Score

71. Is the Customer Information Control System test/monitoring cost justified?
<--- Score

72. What is the standard for acceptable Customer Information Control System performance?
<--- Score

73. Implementation Planning: is a pilot needed to test the changes before a full roll out occurs?
<--- Score

74. Do the Customer Information Control System decisions you make today help people and the

planet tomorrow?
<--- Score

75. How will you measure your QA plan's effectiveness?
<--- Score

76. What is the best design framework for Customer Information Control System organization now that, in a post industrial-age if the top-down, command and control model is no longer relevant?
<--- Score

77. What quality tools were useful in the control phase?
<--- Score

78. Are pertinent alerts monitored, analyzed and distributed to appropriate personnel?
<--- Score

79. Are there documented procedures?
<--- Score

80. Are the planned controls working?
<--- Score

81. What is your theory of human motivation, and how does your compensation plan fit with that view?
<--- Score

82. Have new or revised work instructions resulted?
<--- Score

83. How do your controls stack up?

<--- Score

84. What should the next improvement project be that is related to Customer Information Control System?
<--- Score

85. Is there a Customer Information Control System Communication plan covering who needs to get what information when?
<--- Score

86. Against what alternative is success being measured?
<--- Score

87. What are the critical parameters to watch?
<--- Score

88. How will Customer Information Control System decisions be made and monitored?
<--- Score

89. Who is the Customer Information Control System process owner?
<--- Score

90. Has the Customer Information Control System value of standards been quantified?
<--- Score

91. What are your results for key measures or indicators of the accomplishment of your Customer Information Control System strategy and action plans, including building and strengthening core competencies?

<--- Score

92. What other systems, operations, processes, and infrastructures (hiring practices, staffing, training, incentives/rewards, metrics/dashboards/scorecards, etc.) need updates, additions, changes, or deletions in order to facilitate knowledge transfer and improvements?
<--- Score

93. How might the group capture best practices and lessons learned so as to leverage improvements?
<--- Score

94. How will input, process, and output variables be checked to detect for sub-optimal conditions?
<--- Score

95. Who controls critical resources?
<--- Score

96. How will report readings be checked to effectively monitor performance?
<--- Score

97. How can you best use all of your knowledge repositories to enhance learning and sharing?
<--- Score

98. How do senior leaders actions reflect a commitment to the organizations Customer Information Control System values?
<--- Score

99. How will the day-to-day responsibilities for monitoring and continual improvement be

transferred from the improvement team to the process owner?
<--- Score

100. Who will be in control?
<--- Score

Add up total points for this section:
_____ = Total points for this section

Divided by: _____ (number of statements answered) = _____
Average score for this section

Transfer your score to the Customer Information Control System Index at the beginning of the Self-Assessment.

CRITERION #7: SUSTAIN:

INTENT: Retain the benefits.

In my belief, the answer to this question is clearly defined:

5 Strongly Agree

4 Agree

3 Neutral

2 Disagree

1 Strongly Disagree

1. What you are going to do to affect the numbers?
<--- Score

2. How do you assess the Customer Information Control System pitfalls that are inherent in implementing it?
<--- Score

3. Which functions and people interact with the supplier and or customer?
<--- Score

4. How important is Customer Information Control System to the user organizations mission?
<--- Score

5. Who have you, as a company, historically been when you've been at your best?
<--- Score

6. What happens at your organization when people fail?
<--- Score

7. What stupid rule would you most like to kill?
<--- Score

8. What are the challenges?
<--- Score

9. Are you satisfied with your current role? If not, what is missing from it?
<--- Score

10. What is your competitive advantage?
<--- Score

11. What threat is Customer Information Control System addressing?
<--- Score

12. What Customer Information Control System skills are most important?
<--- Score

13. Are you / should you be revolutionary or evolutionary?

<--- Score

14. Have benefits been optimized with all key stakeholders?
<--- Score

15. Why is it important to have senior management support for a Customer Information Control System project?
<--- Score

16. What unique value proposition (UVP) do you offer?
<--- Score

17. Political -is anyone trying to undermine this project?
<--- Score

18. Who is responsible for errors?
<--- Score

19. How do you ensure that implementations of Customer Information Control System products are done in a way that ensures safety?
<--- Score

20. How do you foster the skills, knowledge, talents, attributes, and characteristics you want to have?
<--- Score

21. What is a feasible sequencing of reform initiatives over time?
<--- Score

22. Is there a work around that you can use?
<--- Score

23. How do you stay inspired?
<--- Score

24. Ask yourself: how would you do this work if you only had one staff member to do it?
<--- Score

25. What are the gaps in your knowledge and experience?
<--- Score

26. What is an unauthorized commitment?
<--- Score

27. What trouble can you get into?
<--- Score

28. If you find that you havent accomplished one of the goals for one of the steps of the Customer Information Control System strategy, what will you do to fix it?
<--- Score

29. Are you relevant? Will you be relevant five years from now? Ten?
<--- Score

30. What have you done to protect your business from competitive encroachment?
<--- Score

31. What are specific Customer Information Control System rules to follow?
<--- Score

32. Why should you adopt a Customer Information Control System framework?

<--- Score

33. What was the last experiment you ran?

<--- Score

34. How do senior leaders deploy your organizations vision and values through your leadership system, to the workforce, to key suppliers and partners, and to customers and other stakeholders, as appropriate?

<--- Score

35. What does your signature ensure?

<--- Score

36. Why will customers want to buy your organizations products/services?

<--- Score

37. Do you feel that more should be done in the Customer Information Control System area?

<--- Score

38. Why should people listen to you?

<--- Score

39. What is the craziest thing you can do?

<--- Score

40. What is the range of capabilities?

<--- Score

41. Who is on the team?

<--- Score

42. What have been your experiences in defining long range Customer Information Control System goals?
<--- Score

43. Who are your customers?
<--- Score

44. What are the potential basics of Customer Information Control System fraud?
<--- Score

45. Is the Customer Information Control System organization completing tasks effectively and efficiently?
<--- Score

46. How do you track customer value, profitability or financial return, organizational success, and sustainability?
<--- Score

47. If you got fired and a new hire took your place, what would she do different?
<--- Score

48. How do you set Customer Information Control System stretch targets and how do you get people to not only participate in setting these stretch targets but also that they strive to achieve these?
<--- Score

49. How can you become the company that would put you out of business?
<--- Score

50. How much contingency will be available in the budget?
<--- Score

51. What is the estimated value of the project?
<--- Score

52. What do we do when new problems arise?
<--- Score

53. Will there be any necessary staff changes (redundancies or new hires)?
<--- Score

54. How will you know that the Customer Information Control System project has been successful?
<--- Score

55. How do you accomplish your long range Customer Information Control System goals?
<--- Score

56. Are all key stakeholders present at all Structured Walkthroughs?
<--- Score

57. Are assumptions made in Customer Information Control System stated explicitly?
<--- Score

58. What is the source of the strategies for Customer Information Control System strengthening and reform?
<--- Score

59. Is Customer Information Control System realistic,

or are you setting yourself up for failure?
<--- Score

60. What is your formula for success in Customer Information Control System ?
<--- Score

61. When information truly is ubiquitous, when reach and connectivity are completely global, when computing resources are infinite, and when a whole new set of impossibilities are not only possible, but happening, what will that do to your business?
<--- Score

62. What is the big Customer Information Control System idea?
<--- Score

63. Do you know what you are doing? And who do you call if you don't?
<--- Score

64. In the past year, what have you done (or could you have done) to increase the accurate perception of your company/brand as ethical and honest?
<--- Score

65. How do you know if you are successful?
<--- Score

66. Who do you think the world wants your organization to be?
<--- Score

67. Are there any activities that you can take off your

to do list?

<--- Score

68. Do you have the right people on the bus?

<--- Score

69. If your company went out of business tomorrow, would anyone who doesn't get a paycheck here care?

<--- Score

70. Why not do Customer Information Control System?

<--- Score

71. If your customer were your grandmother, would you tell her to buy what you're selling?

<--- Score

72. What is the recommended frequency of auditing?

<--- Score

73. Do you have the right capabilities and capacities?

<--- Score

74. Is the impact that Customer Information Control System has shown?

<--- Score

75. How do you listen to customers to obtain actionable information?

<--- Score

76. Which Customer Information Control System goals

are the most important?
<--- Score

77. Whose voice (department, ethnic group, women, older workers, etc) might you have missed hearing from in your company, and how might you amplify this voice to create positive momentum for your business?
<--- Score

78. In a project to restructure Customer Information Control System outcomes, which stakeholders would you involve?
<--- Score

79. What are the short and long-term Customer Information Control System goals?
<--- Score

80. What management system can you use to leverage the Customer Information Control System experience, ideas, and concerns of the people closest to the work to be done?
<--- Score

81. What is the kind of project structure that would be appropriate for your Customer Information Control System project, should it be formal and complex, or can it be less formal and relatively simple?
<--- Score

82. Can you break it down?
<--- Score

83. What happens when a new employee joins the organization?

<--- Score

84. What would you recommend your friend do if he/ she were facing this dilemma?
<--- Score

85. Did your employees make progress today?
<--- Score

86. Who uses your product in ways you never expected?
<--- Score

87. Who is the main stakeholder, with ultimate responsibility for driving Customer Information Control System forward?
<--- Score

88. How much does Customer Information Control System help?
<--- Score

89. How do you lead with Customer Information Control System in mind?
<--- Score

90. Who will be responsible for deciding whether Customer Information Control System goes ahead or not after the initial investigations?
<--- Score

91. How do you provide a safe environment -physically and emotionally?
<--- Score

92. How long will it take to change?

<--- Score

93. Has implementation been effective in reaching specified objectives so far?
<--- Score

94. What knowledge, skills and characteristics mark a good Customer Information Control System project manager?
<--- Score

95. Are the criteria for selecting recommendations stated?
<--- Score

96. How do you govern and fulfill your societal responsibilities?
<--- Score

97. Have new benefits been realized?
<--- Score

98. Who, on the executive team or the board, has spoken to a customer recently?
<--- Score

99. How can you negotiate Customer Information Control System successfully with a stubborn boss, an irate client, or a deceitful coworker?
<--- Score

100. Who do we want your customers to become?
<--- Score

101. Is maximizing Customer Information Control System protection the same as minimizing

Customer Information Control System loss?
<--- Score

102. If you do not follow, then how to lead?
<--- Score

103. What is the purpose of Customer Information Control System in relation to the mission?
<--- Score

104. How do customers see your organization?
<--- Score

105. How do you go about securing Customer Information Control System?
<--- Score

106. What trophy do you want on your mantle?
<--- Score

107. How do you foster innovation?
<--- Score

108. What are your most important goals for the strategic Customer Information Control System objectives?
<--- Score

109. Are the assumptions believable and achievable?
<--- Score

110. Do you think you know, or do you know you know ?
<--- Score

111. Who will manage the integration of tools?
<--- Score

112. How do you deal with Customer Information Control System changes?
<--- Score

113. Whom among your colleagues do you trust, and for what?
<--- Score

114. What Customer Information Control System modifications can you make work for you?
<--- Score

115. What are current Customer Information Control System paradigms?
<--- Score

116. What are you challenging?
<--- Score

117. Were lessons learned captured and communicated?
<--- Score

118. What is your question? Why?
<--- Score

119. What one word do you want to own in the minds of your customers, employees, and partners?
<--- Score

120. What counts that you are not counting?
<--- Score

121. What relationships among Customer Information Control System trends do you perceive?

<--- Score

122. Think of your Customer Information Control System project, what are the main functions?

<--- Score

123. Is Customer Information Control System dependent on the successful delivery of a current project?

<--- Score

124. Marketing budgets are tighter, consumers are more skeptical, and social media has changed forever the way we talk about Customer Information Control System, how do you gain traction?

<--- Score

125. Is there any reason to believe the opposite of my current belief?

<--- Score

126. Would you rather sell to knowledgeable and informed customers or to uninformed customers?

<--- Score

127. How do you maintain Customer Information Control System's Integrity?

<--- Score

128. Who is responsible for ensuring appropriate resources (time, people and money) are allocated to Customer Information Control System?

<--- Score

129. Are you using a design thinking approach and integrating Innovation, Customer Information Control System Experience, and Brand Value?
<--- Score

130. What is the overall talent health of your organization as a whole at senior levels, and for each organization reporting to a member of the Senior Leadership Team?
<--- Score

131. If you weren't already in this business, would you enter it today? And if not, what are you going to do about it?
<--- Score

132. Are you making progress, and are you making progress as Customer Information Control System leaders?
<--- Score

133. Are you changing as fast as the world around you?
<--- Score

134. What information is critical to your organization that your executives are ignoring?
<--- Score

135. Do you have enough freaky customers in your portfolio pushing you to the limit day in and day out?
<--- Score

136. Which models, tools and techniques are necessary?
<--- Score

137. Are your responses positive or negative?
<--- Score

138. Can you maintain your growth without detracting from the factors that have contributed to your success?
<--- Score

139. Operational - will it work?
<--- Score

140. How do you make it meaningful in connecting Customer Information Control System with what users do day-to-day?
<--- Score

141. What is your Customer Information Control System strategy?
<--- Score

142. Are you paying enough attention to the partners your company depends on to succeed?
<--- Score

143. How do you determine the key elements that affect Customer Information Control System workforce satisfaction, how are these elements determined for different workforce groups and segments?
<--- Score

144. Is it economical; do you have the time and money?
<--- Score

145. What new services of functionality will be implemented next with Customer Information Control System ?
<--- Score

146. Do you say no to customers for no reason?
<--- Score

147. What are the top 3 things at the forefront of your Customer Information Control System agendas for the next 3 years?
<--- Score

148. Do you have past Customer Information Control System successes?
<--- Score

149. What is effective Customer Information Control System?
<--- Score

150. Who are four people whose careers you have enhanced?
<--- Score

151. How do you cross-sell and up-sell your Customer Information Control System success?
<--- Score

152. Who else should you help?
<--- Score

153. Will it be accepted by users?
<--- Score

154. If there were zero limitations, what would you

do differently?

<--- Score

155. Where can you break convention?

<--- Score

156. Do you have an implicit bias for capital investments over people investments?

<--- Score

157. Are you maintaining a past–present–future perspective throughout the Customer Information Control System discussion?

<--- Score

158. How does Customer Information Control System integrate with other stakeholder initiatives?

<--- Score

159. Who are the key stakeholders?

<--- Score

160. What are the essentials of internal Customer Information Control System management?

<--- Score

161. What are the barriers to increased Customer Information Control System production?

<--- Score

162. Do Customer Information Control System rules make a reasonable demand on a users capabilities?

<--- Score

163. Can the schedule be done in the given time?

<--- Score

164. What could happen if you do not do it?
<--- Score

165. Who will determine interim and final deadlines?
<--- Score

166. To whom do you add value?
<--- Score

167. What are the success criteria that will indicate that Customer Information Control System objectives have been met and the benefits delivered?
<--- Score

168. What happens if you do not have enough funding?
<--- Score

169. What should you stop doing?
<--- Score

170. Who will provide the final approval of Customer Information Control System deliverables?
<--- Score

171. What are the rules and assumptions your industry operates under? What if the opposite were true?
<--- Score

172. Do you think Customer Information Control System accomplishes the goals you expect it to accomplish?
<--- Score

173. In retrospect, of the projects that you pulled the plug on, what percent do you wish had been allowed to keep going, and what percent do you wish had ended earlier?
<--- Score

174. What would have to be true for the option on the table to be the best possible choice?
<--- Score

175. If you had to rebuild your organization without any traditional competitive advantages (i.e., no killer technology, promising research, innovative product/service delivery model, etcetera), how would your people have to approach their work and collaborate together in order to create the necessary conditions for success?
<--- Score

176. What potential megatrends could make your business model obsolete?
<--- Score

177. What are the key enablers to make this Customer Information Control System move?
<--- Score

178. Do you see more potential in people than they do in themselves?
<--- Score

179. What projects are going on in the organization today, and what resources are those projects using from the resource pools?
<--- Score

180. If you were responsible for initiating and implementing major changes in your organization, what steps might you take to ensure acceptance of those changes?
<--- Score

181. Do you know who is a friend or a foe?
<--- Score

182. How can you become more high-tech but still be high touch?
<--- Score

183. What are the usability implications of Customer Information Control System actions?
<--- Score

184. What are the long-term Customer Information Control System goals?
<--- Score

185. How do you manage Customer Information Control System Knowledge Management (KM)?
<--- Score

186. How likely is it that a customer would recommend your company to a friend or colleague?
<--- Score

187. How can you incorporate support to ensure safe and effective use of Customer Information Control System into the services that you provide?
<--- Score

188. How is implementation research currently

incorporated into each of your goals?
<--- Score

189. What are you trying to prove to yourself, and how might it be hijacking your life and business success?
<--- Score

190. What is your BATNA (best alternative to a negotiated agreement)?
<--- Score

191. Is your strategy driving your strategy? Or is the way in which you allocate resources driving your strategy?
<--- Score

192. What will be the consequences to the stakeholder (financial, reputation etc) if Customer Information Control System does not go ahead or fails to deliver the objectives?
<--- Score

193. What business benefits will Customer Information Control System goals deliver if achieved?
<--- Score

194. What is it like to work for you?
<--- Score

195. What is the overall business strategy?
<--- Score

196. How do you keep the momentum going?
<--- Score

197. If no one would ever find out about your

accomplishments, how would you lead differently?
<--- Score

198. How do you create buy-in?
<--- Score

199. What may be the consequences for the performance of an organization if all stakeholders are not consulted regarding Customer Information Control System?
<--- Score

200. Why do and why don't your customers like your organization?
<--- Score

201. How will you insure seamless interoperability of Customer Information Control System moving forward?
<--- Score

202. Is there any existing Customer Information Control System governance structure?
<--- Score

203. How will you ensure you get what you expected?
<--- Score

204. Is your basic point _____ or _____?
<--- Score

205. What are strategies for increasing support and reducing opposition?
<--- Score

206. What goals did you miss?

<--- Score

207. What role does communication play in the success or failure of a Customer Information Control System project?
<--- Score

208. Is a Customer Information Control System breakthrough on the horizon?
<--- Score

209. How do you transition from the baseline to the target?
<--- Score

210. Can you do all this work?
<--- Score

211. What must you excel at?
<--- Score

212. How will you motivate the stakeholders with the least vested interest?
<--- Score

213. Are new benefits received and understood?
<--- Score

214. At what moment would you think; Will I get fired?
<--- Score

215. Which individuals, teams or departments will be involved in Customer Information Control System?
<--- Score

216. How are you doing compared to your industry?
<--- Score

Add up total points for this section:
_ _ _ _ _ = Total points for this section

Divided by: _ _ _ _ _ _ (number of statements answered) = _ _ _ _ _ _
Average score for this section

Transfer your score to the Customer Information Control System Index at the beginning of the Self-Assessment.

Customer Information Control System and Managing Projects, Criteria for Project Managers:

1.0 Initiating Process Group: Customer Information Control System

1. Were decisions made in a timely manner?

2. What were the challenges that you encountered during the execution of a previous Customer Information Control System project that you would not want to repeat?

3. How will it affect me?

4. Where must it be done?

5. Does it make any difference if you am successful?

6. Although the Customer Information Control System project manager does not directly manage procurement and contracting activities, who does manage procurement and contracting activities in your organization then if not the PM?

7. Do you know the roles & responsibilities required for this Customer Information Control System project?

8. What communication items need improvement?

9. Are the Customer Information Control System project team and stakeholders meeting regularly and using a meeting agenda and taking notes to accurately document what is being covered and what happened in the weekly meetings?

10. Contingency planning. if a risk event occurs, what will you do?

11. What were things that you did well, and could improve, and how?

12. Which six sigma dmaic phase focuses on why and how defects and errors occur?

13. What are the constraints?

14. Who is funding the Customer Information Control System project?

15. Do you know all the stakeholders impacted by the Customer Information Control System project and what needs are?

16. Based on your Customer Information Control System project communication management plan, what worked well?

17. What will you do to minimize the impact should a risk event occur?

18. When must it be done?

19. What were things that you need to improve?

20. What are the inputs required to produce the deliverables?

1.1 Project Charter: Customer Information Control System

21. Why is a Customer Information Control System project Charter used?

22. How much?

23. Why the improvements?

24. Dependent Customer Information Control System projects: what Customer Information Control System projects must be underway or completed before this Customer Information Control System project can be successful?

25. Are there special technology requirements?

26. Avoid costs, improve service, and/ or comply with a mandate?

27. Who is the Customer Information Control System project Manager?

28. For whom?

29. Are you building in-house ?

30. What are the assigned resources?

31. Will this replace an existing product?

32. How high should you set your goals?

33. What is the most common tool for helping define the detail?

34. What are you trying to accomplish?

35. Assumptions: what factors, for planning purposes, are you considering to be true?

36. Why do you need to manage scope?

37. Where does all this information come from?

38. Where and how does the team fit within your organization structure?

39. Customer benefits: what customer requirements does this Customer Information Control System project address?

40. Who ise input and support will this Customer Information Control System project require?

1.2 Stakeholder Register: Customer Information Control System

41. Is your organization ready for change?

42. What & Why?

43. What are the major Customer Information Control System project milestones requiring communications or providing communications opportunities?

44. How should employers make voices heard?

45. Who are the stakeholders?

46. Who wants to talk about Security?

47. What opportunities exist to provide communications?

48. How will reports be created?

49. How much influence do they have on the Customer Information Control System project?

50. What is the power of the stakeholder?

51. Who is managing stakeholder engagement?

52. How big is the gap?

1.3 Stakeholder Analysis Matrix: Customer Information Control System

53. Legislative effects?

54. Global influences?

55. What do you Evaluate?

56. Sustaining internal capabilities?

57. Organizational Applicability?

58. Environmental effects?

59. Are there two or three that rise to the top, and a couple that are sliding to the bottom?

60. Who determines value?

61. What is your organizations competitors doing?

62. Tactics: eg, surprise, major contracts?

63. Lack of competitive strength?

64. Beneficiaries; who are the potential beneficiaries?

65. Who is most dependent on the resources at stake?

66. Management cover, succession?

67. Do any safeguard policies apply to the Customer

Information Control System project?

68. Will the impacts be local, national or international?

69. Loss of key staff?

70. Is there evidence that demonstrates the impact of education on the Customer Information Control System projects outcomes?

71. How to measure the achievement of the Immediate Objective?

72. Market developments?

2.0 Planning Process Group: Customer Information Control System

73. What good practices or successful experiences or transferable examples have been identified?

74. Does it make any difference if you are successful?

75. The Customer Information Control System project charter is created in which Customer Information Control System project management process group?

76. What makes your Customer Information Control System project successful?

77. Is your organization showing technical capacity and leadership commitment to keep working with the Customer Information Control System project and to repeat it?

78. Are work methodologies, financial instruments, etc. shared among departments, organizations and Customer Information Control System projects?

79. On which process should team members spend the most time?

80. You did your readings, yes?

81. First of all, should any action be taken?

82. What do you need to do?

83. Customer Information Control System project assessment; why did you do this Customer Information Control System project?

84. To what extent have public/private national resources and/or counterparts been mobilized to contribute to the programs objective and produce results and impacts?

85. How can you tell when you are done?

86. To what extent has the intervention strategy been adapted to the areas of intervention in which it is being implemented?

87. Are there efficient coordination mechanisms to avoid overloading the counterparts, participating stakeholders?

88. In what way has the Customer Information Control System project come up with innovative measures for problem-solving?

89. Have more efficient (sensitive) and appropriate measures been adopted to respond to the political and socio-cultural problems identified?

90. How will you do it?

91. Does the program have follow-up mechanisms (to verify the quality of the products, punctuality of delivery, etc.) to measure progress in the achievement of the envisaged results?

92. What business situation is being addressed?

2.1 Project Management Plan: Customer Information Control System

93. What is risk management?

94. What would you do differently what did not work?

95. Was the peer (technical) review of the cost estimates duly coordinated with the cost estimate center of expertise and addressed in the review documentation and certification?

96. Why Change?

97. What is the business need?

98. Are there non-structural buyout or relocation recommendations?

99. Do the proposed changes from the Customer Information Control System project include any significant risks to safety?

100. If the Customer Information Control System project management plan is a comprehensive document that guides you in Customer Information Control System project execution and control, then what should it NOT contain?

101. Who is the Customer Information Control System project Manager?

102. What would you do differently?

103. What does management expect of PMs?

104. What if, for example, the positive direction and vision of your organization causes expected trends to change resulting in greater need than expected?

105. Are the existing and future without-plan conditions reasonable and appropriate?

106. Are there any client staffing expectations?

107. Does the selected plan protect privacy?

108. What are the training needs?

109. What data/reports/tools/etc. do program managers need?

110. Has the selected plan been formulated using cost effectiveness and incremental analysis techniques?

2.2 Scope Management Plan: Customer Information Control System

111. Has the Customer Information Control System project manager been identified?

112. Are Customer Information Control System project contact logs kept up to date?

113. Who is responsible for monitoring the Customer Information Control System project scope to ensure the Customer Information Control System project remains within the scope baseline?

114. Has a capability assessment been conducted?

115. What is your organizations history in doing similar activities?

116. Have the procedures for identifying budget variances been followed?

117. Will the Customer Information Control System project deliverables become accepted in writing?

118. What happens to rejected deliverables?

119. Process groups – where do scope management processes fit in?

120. Are you doing what you have set out to do?

121. Is a pmo (Customer Information Control System

project management office) in place and provide oversight to the Customer Information Control System project?

122. Does the Customer Information Control System project have a Statement of Work?

123. Pop quiz – which are the same inputs as in scope planning?

124. What is the need the Customer Information Control System project will address?

125. Do Customer Information Control System project managers participating in the Customer Information Control System project know the Customer Information Control System projects true status first hand?

126. Does the Customer Information Control System project team have the skills necessary to successfully complete current Customer Information Control System project(s) and support the application?

127. Has a resource management plan been created?

128. Are assumptions being identified, recorded, analyzed, qualified and closed?

129. Cost / benefit analysis?

130. Are there any windfall benefits that would accrue to the Customer Information Control System project sponsor or other parties?

2.3 Requirements Management Plan: Customer Information Control System

131. Who will finally present the work or product(s) for acceptance?

132. Has the requirements team been instructed in the Change Control process?

133. How knowledgeable is the primary Stakeholder(s) in the proposed application area?

134. Business analysis scope?

135. Did you avoid subjective, flowery or non-specific statements?

136. How detailed should the Customer Information Control System project get?

137. Are actual resource expenditures versus planned still acceptable?

138. Do you understand the role that each stakeholder will play in the requirements process?

139. Is the change control process documented?

140. Do you really need to write this document at all?

141. Do you know which stakeholders will participate in the requirements effort?

142. Does the Customer Information Control System project have a Change Control process?

143. Will the Customer Information Control System project requirements become approved in writing?

144. Who has the authority to reject Customer Information Control System project requirements?

145. After the requirements are gathered and set forth on the requirements register, theyre little more than a laundry list of items. Some may be duplicates, some might conflict with others and some will be too broad or too vague to understand. Describe how the requirements will be analyzed. Who will perform the analysis?

146. Did you provide clear and concise specifications?

147. Who will approve the requirements (and if multiple approvers, in what order)?

148. Is it new or replacing an existing business system or process?

149. To see if a requirement statement is sufficiently well-defined, read it from the developers perspective. Mentally add the phrase, call me when youre done to the end of the requirement and see if that makes you nervous. In other words, would you need additional clarification from the author to understand the requirement well enough to design and implement it?

150. Should you include sub-activities?

2.4 Requirements Documentation: Customer Information Control System

151. Are there legal issues?

152. What happens when requirements are wrong?

153. What are the potential disadvantages/advantages?

154. Are there any requirements conflicts?

155. Where do system and software requirements come from, what are sources?

156. What facilities must be supported by the system?

157. How does the proposed Customer Information Control System project contribute to the overall objectives of your organization?

158. What kind of entity is a problem ?

159. Consistency. are there any requirements conflicts?

160. Who is interacting with the system?

161. How much testing do you need to do to prove that your system is safe?

162. Where do you define what is a customer, what are the attributes of customer?

163. What is the risk associated with cost and schedule?

164. Is the origin of the requirement clearly stated?

165. If applicable; are there issues linked with the fact that this is an offshore Customer Information Control System project?

166. How do you know when a Requirement is accurate enough?

167. Is new technology needed?

168. What is a show stopper in the requirements?

169. What are current process problems?

170. Does the system provide the functions which best support the customers needs?

2.5 Requirements Traceability Matrix: Customer Information Control System

171. What is the WBS?

172. Do you have a clear understanding of all subcontracts in place?

173. Why do you manage scope?

174. Will you use a Requirements Traceability Matrix?

175. Describe the process for approving requirements so they can be added to the traceability matrix and Customer Information Control System project work can be performed. Will the Customer Information Control System project requirements become approved in writing?

176. What percentage of Customer Information Control System projects are producing traceability matrices between requirements and other work products?

177. What are the chronologies, contingencies, consequences, criteria?

178. Is there a requirements traceability process in place?

179. Why use a WBS?

180. How small is small enough?

181. How do you manage scope?

182. How will it affect the stakeholders personally in career?

2.6 Project Scope Statement: Customer Information Control System

183. Elements of scope management that deal with concept development ?

184. Elements that deal with providing the detail?

185. Have you been able to easily identify success criteria and create objective measurements for each of the Customer Information Control System project scopes goal statements?

186. Are the meetings set up to have assigned note takers that will add action/issues to the issue list?

187. Risks?

188. Will this process be communicated to the customer and Customer Information Control System project team?

189. Will the risk plan be updated on a regular and frequent basis?

190. What are the possible consequences should a risk come to occur?

191. Did your Customer Information Control System project ask for this?

192. If you were to write a list of what should not be included in the scope statement, what are the things

that you would recommend be described as out-of-scope?

193. If there are vendors, have they signed off on the Customer Information Control System project Plan?

194. Will the risk status be reported to management on a regular and frequent basis?

195. What is change?

196. Is there a Quality Assurance Plan documented and filed?

197. Relevant - ask yourself can you get there; why are you doing this Customer Information Control System project?

198. What actions will be taken to mitigate the risk?

199. If there is an independent oversight contractor, have they signed off on the Customer Information Control System project Plan?

2.7 Assumption and Constraint Log: Customer Information Control System

200. What other teams / processes would be impacted by changes to the current process, and how?

201. Does the plan conform to standards?

202. Have Customer Information Control System project management standards and procedures been established and documented?

203. Are there cosmetic errors that hinder readability and comprehension?

204. How do you design an auditing system?

205. Have you eliminated all duplicative tasks or manual efforts, where appropriate?

206. Have all necessary approvals been obtained?

207. Have adequate resources been provided by management to ensure Customer Information Control System project success?

208. After observing execution of process, is it in compliance with the documented Plan?

209. Do you know what your customers expectations are regarding this process?

210. What weaknesses do you have?

211. Are best practices and metrics employed to identify issues, progress, performance, etc.?

212. Does a documented Customer Information Control System project organizational policy & plan (i.e. governance model) exist?

213. Have all stakeholders been identified?

214. Can you perform this task or activity in a more effective manner?

215. If it is out of compliance, should the process be amended or should the Plan be amended?

216. What is positive about the current process?

217. Was the document/deliverable developed per the appropriate or required standards (for example, Institute of Electrical and Electronics Engineers standards)?

218. What strengths do you have?

2.8 Work Breakdown Structure: Customer Information Control System

219. Is it a change in scope?

220. When does it have to be done?

221. How big is a work-package?

222. What is the probability of completing the Customer Information Control System project in less that xx days?

223. How much detail?

224. Is it still viable?

225. Is the work breakdown structure (wbs) defined and is the scope of the Customer Information Control System project clear with assigned deliverable owners?

226. Do you need another level?

227. What has to be done?

228. Who has to do it?

229. How many levels?

230. When do you stop?

231. Why is it useful?

232. Can you make it?

233. How far down?

234. Where does it take place?

2.9 WBS Dictionary: Customer Information Control System

235. Major functional areas of contract effort?

236. Are meaningful indicators identified for use in measuring the status of cost and schedule performance?

237. Are retroactive changes to BCWS and BCWP prohibited except for correction of errors or for normal accounting adjustments?

238. Are records maintained to show how undistributed budgets are controlled?

239. Are direct or indirect cost adjustments being accomplished according to accounting procedures acceptable to us?

240. Does the contractors system include procedures for measuring the performance of critical subcontractors?

241. Budgeted cost for work performed?

242. Does the contractors system provide for the determination of cost variances attributable to the excess usage of material?

243. Are overhead cost budgets (or Customer Information Control System projections) established on a facility-wide basis at least annually for the life of

the contract?

244. Do procedures specify under what circumstances replanning of open work packages may occur, and the methods to be followed?

245. Do work packages reflect the actual way in which the work will be done and are they meaningful products or management-oriented subdivisions of a higher level element of work?

246. Are retroactive changes to direct costs and indirect costs prohibited except for the correction of errors and routine accounting adjustments?

247. Are the overhead pools formally and adequately identified?

248. Is cost performance measurement at the point in time most suitable for the category of material involved, and no earlier than the time of actual receipt of material?

249. Does the contractors system description or procedures require that the performance measurement baseline plus management reserve equal the contract budget base?

250. Does the contractor use objective results, design reviews and tests to trace schedule performance?

251. Are all affected work authorizations, budgeting, and scheduling documents amended to properly reflect the effects of authorized changes?

252. Changes in the overhead pool and/or

organization structures?

253. Are procedures in existence that control replanning of unopened work packages, and are corresponding procedures adhered to?

2.10 Schedule Management Plan: Customer Information Control System

254. Are the activity durations realistic and at an appropriate level of detail for effective management?

255. Goal: is the schedule feasible and at what cost?

256. Is the schedule updated on a periodic basis?

257. Personnel with expertise?

258. Are the primary and secondary schedule tools defined?

259. Staffing Requirements?

260. Does the detailed work plan match the complexity of tasks with the capabilities of personnel?

261. Have key stakeholders been identified?

262. Are the people assigned to the Customer Information Control System project sufficiently qualified?

263. Are the key elements of a Customer Information Control System project Charter present?

264. Has the budget been baselined?

265. Are there any activities or deliverables being added or gold-plated that could be dropped or scaled

back without falling short of the original requirement?

266. Will the Customer Information Control System project sponsor be involved in preliminary schedule reviews?

267. Is there a procedure for management, control and release of schedule margin?

268. Is there anything planned that does not need to be here?

269. Is a process defined for baseline approval and control?

270. Are non-critical path items updated and agreed upon with the teams?

271. Does all Customer Information Control System project documentation reside in a common repository for easy access?

272. Does the Customer Information Control System project have a Quality Culture?

273. Do all stakeholders know how to access this repository and where to find the Customer Information Control System project documentation?

2.11 Activity List: Customer Information Control System

274. The wbs is developed as part of a joint planning session. and how do you know that youhave done this right?

275. How detailed should a Customer Information Control System project get?

276. What is the LF and LS for each activity?

277. In what sequence?

278. How difficult will it be to do specific activities on this Customer Information Control System project?

279. What went wrong?

280. How should ongoing costs be monitored to try to keep the Customer Information Control System project within budget?

281. How will it be performed?

282. For other activities, how much delay can be tolerated?

283. What went well?

284. Is infrastructure setup part of your Customer Information Control System project?

285. Where will it be performed?

286. What are you counting on?

287. How much slack is available in the Customer Information Control System project?

288. What are the critical bottleneck activities?

289. What did not go as well?

290. Are the required resources available or need to be acquired?

291. How do you determine the late start (LS) for each activity?

2.12 Activity Attributes: Customer Information Control System

292. How else could the items be grouped?

293. Are the required resources available?

294. Activity: fair or not fair?

295. Has management defined a definite timeframe for the turnaround or Customer Information Control System project window?

296. Do you feel very comfortable with your prediction?

297. How difficult will it be to complete specific activities on this Customer Information Control System project?

298. What conclusions/generalizations can you draw from this?

299. Activity: what is In the Bag?

300. Activity: what is Missing?

301. How much activity detail is required?

302. What is the general pattern here?

303. Resources to accomplish the work?

304. Is there a trend during the year?

305. Which method produces the more accurate cost assignment?

306. What activity do you think you should spend the most time on?

307. Were there other ways you could have organized the data to achieve similar results?

308. What is missing?

2.13 Milestone List: Customer Information Control System

309. Reliability of data, plan predictability?

310. Marketing - reach, distribution, awareness?

311. What would happen if a delivery of material was one week late?

312. Vital contracts and partners?

313. How do you manage time?

314. Describe your organizations strengths and core competencies. What factors will make your organization succeed?

315. Who will manage the Customer Information Control System project on a day-to-day basis?

316. Obstacles faced?

317. Information and research?

318. Effects on core activities, distraction?

319. Milestone pages should display the UserID of the person who added the milestone. Does a report or query exist that provides this audit information?

320. Describe the concept of the technology, product or service that will be or has been developed. How

will it be used?

321. New USPs?

322. Do you foresee any technical risks or developmental challenges?

323. What date will the task finish?

324. Identify critical paths (one or more) and which activities are on the critical path?

2.14 Network Diagram: Customer Information Control System

325. If the Customer Information Control System project network diagram cannot change and you have extra personnel resources, what is the BEST thing to do?

326. What must be completed before an activity can be started?

327. If a current contract exists, can you provide the vendor name, contract start, and contract expiration date?

328. Will crashing x weeks return more in benefits than it costs?

329. What can be done concurrently?

330. What are the Major Administrative Issues?

331. Are you on time?

332. Where do you schedule uncertainty time?

333. What job or jobs could run concurrently?

334. What is the probability of completing the Customer Information Control System project in less that xx days?

335. What job or jobs precede it?

336. Are the gantt chart and/or network diagram updated periodically and used to assess the overall Customer Information Control System project timetable?

337. Which type of network diagram allows you to depict four types of dependencies?

338. What job or jobs follow it?

339. How confident can you be in your milestone dates and the delivery date?

340. What are the Key Success Factors?

341. How difficult will it be to do specific activities on this Customer Information Control System project?

342. What is the lowest cost to complete this Customer Information Control System project in xx weeks?

2.15 Activity Resource Requirements: Customer Information Control System

343. Do you use tools like decomposition and rolling-wave planning to produce the activity list and other outputs?

344. What are constraints that you might find during the Human Resource Planning process?

345. How many signatures do you require on a check and does this match what is in your policy and procedures?

346. Are there unresolved issues that need to be addressed?

347. Anything else?

348. Time for overtime?

349. Which logical relationship does the PDM use most often?

350. Other support in specific areas?

351. What is the Work Plan Standard?

352. How do you handle petty cash?

353. When does monitoring begin?

354. Why do you do that?

2.16 Resource Breakdown Structure: Customer Information Control System

355. Who will be used as a Customer Information Control System project team member?

356. Why time management?

357. What can you do to improve productivity?

358. What are the requirements for resource data?

359. What is Customer Information Control System project communication management?

360. What went right?

361. Goals for the Customer Information Control System project. What is each stakeholders desired outcome for the Customer Information Control System project?

362. Who is allowed to perform which functions?

363. What is each stakeholders desired outcome for the Customer Information Control System project?

364. What defines a successful Customer Information Control System project?

365. Why do you do it?

366. Changes based on input from stakeholders?

367. What is the difference between % Complete and % work?

368. How difficult will it be to do specific activities on this Customer Information Control System project?

369. Is predictive resource analysis being done?

370. Who is allowed to see what data about which resources?

371. Which resources should be in the resource pool?

2.17 Activity Duration Estimates: Customer Information Control System

372. Which type of mathematical analysis is being used?

373. What type of information goes in a quality assurance plan?

374. What should be done NEXT?

375. What is the duration of a milestone?

376. It under budget or over budget?

377. Does a process exist to identify which qualified resources may be attainable?

378. Did anything besides luck make a difference between success and failure?

379. Is the cost performance monitored to identify variances from the plan?

380. Does a process exist to determine which risk events to accept and which events to disregard?

381. Are measurement techniques employed to determine the potential impact of proposed changes?

382. Are Customer Information Control System project records organized, maintained, and assessable by Customer Information Control System project team

members?

383. What does it mean to take a systems view of a Customer Information Control System project?

384. Are risks that are likely to affect the Customer Information Control System project identified and documented?

385. What is pmp certification, and why do you think the number of people earning it has grown so much in the past ten years?

386. See what went wrong?

387. Why do you need a good WBS to use Customer Information Control System project management software?

388. How does Customer Information Control System project integration management relate to the Customer Information Control System project life cycle, stakeholders, and the other Customer Information Control System project management knowledge areas?

389. Do they make sense?

390. What is involved in the solicitation process?

2.18 Duration Estimating Worksheet: Customer Information Control System

391. Is this operation cost effective?

392. What questions do you have?

393. What info is needed?

394. What is cost and Customer Information Control System project cost management?

395. How can the Customer Information Control System project be displayed graphically to better visualize the activities?

396. Is the Customer Information Control System project responsive to community need?

397. Does the Customer Information Control System project provide innovative ways for stakeholders to overcome obstacles or deliver better outcomes?

398. What utility impacts are there?

399. How should ongoing costs be monitored to try to keep the Customer Information Control System project within budget?

400. Is a construction detail attached (to aid in explanation)?

401. Define the work as completely as possible. What

work will be included in the Customer Information Control System project?

402. Do any colleagues have experience with your organization and/or RFPs?

403. What work will be included in the Customer Information Control System project?

404. What is your role?

405. What is the total time required to complete the Customer Information Control System project if no delays occur?

2.19 Project Schedule: Customer Information Control System

406. Have all Customer Information Control System project delays been adequately accounted for, communicated to all stakeholders and adjustments made in overall Customer Information Control System project schedule?

407. Schedule/cost recovery?

408. What is risk?

409. How can you shorten the schedule?

410. Why do you need to manage Customer Information Control System project Risk?

411. To what degree is do you feel the entire team was committed to the Customer Information Control System project schedule?

412. Are you working on the right risks?

413. Month Customer Information Control System project take?

414. Are key risk mitigation strategies added to the Customer Information Control System project schedule?

415. Should you have a test for each code module?

416. How can slack be negative?

417. Is Customer Information Control System project work proceeding in accordance with the original Customer Information Control System project schedule?

418. Understand the constraints used in preparing the schedule. Are activities connected because logic dictates the order in which others occur?

419. How do you manage Customer Information Control System project Risk?

420. Did the Customer Information Control System project come in on schedule?

421. Customer Information Control System project work estimates Who is managing the work estimate quality of work tasks in the Customer Information Control System project schedule?

422. Meet requirements?

423. Are there activities that came from a template or previous Customer Information Control System project that are not applicable on this phase of this Customer Information Control System project?

424. How does a Customer Information Control System project get to be a year late ?

2.20 Cost Management Plan: Customer Information Control System

425. Are key risk mitigation strategies added to the Customer Information Control System project schedule?

426. What is the work breakdown structure for the Customer Information Control System project?

427. Responsibilities – what is the split of responsibilities between the owner and contractors?

428. Are Customer Information Control System project leaders committed to this Customer Information Control System project full time?

429. Are multiple estimation methods being employed?

430. Scope of work – What is the scope of work for each of the planned contracts?

431. Have activity relationships and interdependencies within tasks been adequately identified?

432. Cost estimate preparation – What cost estimates will be prepared during the Customer Information Control System project phases?

433. Does the business case include how the Customer Information Control System project aligns

with your organizations strategic goals & objectives?

434. Is there an onboarding process in place?

435. Has Customer Information Control System project success criteria been defined?

436. Is a pmo (Customer Information Control System project management office) in place and provide oversight to the Customer Information Control System project?

437. Resources – how will human resources be scheduled during each phase of the Customer Information Control System project?

438. Risk rating?

439. Are Customer Information Control System project contact logs kept up to date?

440. Have all documents been archived in a Customer Information Control System project repository for each release?

441. For cost control purposes?

442. Do all stakeholders know how to access this repository and where to find the Customer Information Control System project documentation?

2.21 Activity Cost Estimates: Customer Information Control System

443. What makes a good expected result statement?

444. What happens if you cannot produce the documentation for the single audit?

445. Are data needed on characteristics of care?

446. How many activities should you have?

447. Does the activity rely on a common set of tools to carry it out?

448. How difficult will it be to do specific tasks on the Customer Information Control System project?

449. Padding is bad and contingencies are good. what is the difference?

450. What is your organizations history in doing similar tasks?

451. How do you fund change orders?

452. The impact and what actions were taken?

453. How do you manage cost?

454. Who & what determines the need for contracted services?

455. How quickly can the task be done with the skills available?

456. Would you hire them again?

457. What makes a good activity description?

458. Will you use any tools, such as Customer Information Control System project management software, to assist in capturing Earned Value metrics?

459. How Award?

2.22 Cost Estimating Worksheet: Customer Information Control System

460. Ask: are others positioned to know, are others credible, and will others cooperate?

461. What happens to any remaining funds not used?

462. What costs are to be estimated?

463. What is the purpose of estimating?

464. What is the estimated labor cost today based upon this information?

465. Identify the timeframe necessary to monitor progress and collect data to determine how the selected measure has changed?

466. Can a trend be established from historical performance data on the selected measure and are the criteria for using trend analysis or forecasting methods met?

467. What can be included?

468. What will others want?

469. What additional Customer Information Control System project(s) could be initiated as a result of this Customer Information Control System project?

470. Who is best positioned to know and assist in

identifying corresponding factors?

471. Will the Customer Information Control System project collaborate with the local community and leverage resources?

472. Does the Customer Information Control System project provide innovative ways for stakeholders to overcome obstacles or deliver better outcomes?

473. How will the results be shared and to whom?

474. Value pocket identification & quantification what are value pockets?

475. Is it feasible to establish a control group arrangement?

476. Is the Customer Information Control System project responsive to community need?

2.23 Cost Baseline: Customer Information Control System

477. Customer Information Control System project goals -should others be reconsidered?

478. How accurate do cost estimates need to be?

479. Should a more thorough impact analysis be conducted?

480. Have the lessons learned been filed with the Customer Information Control System project Management Office?

481. Have all approved changes to the cost baseline been identified and impact on the Customer Information Control System project documented?

482. Is the requested change request a result of changes in other Customer Information Control System project(s)?

483. Has the Customer Information Control System projected annual cost to operate and maintain the product(s) or service(s) been approved and funded?

484. Impact to environment?

485. Have the actual milestone completion dates been compared to the approved schedule?

486. Will the Customer Information Control System

project fail if the change request is not executed?

487. How will cost estimates be used?

488. Has operations management formally accepted responsibility for operating and maintaining the product(s) or service(s) delivered by the Customer Information Control System project?

489. Escalation criteria met?

490. Is request in line with priorities?

491. What is the reality?

492. On budget?

493. What does a good WBS NOT look like?

494. Has the appropriate access to relevant data and analysis capability been granted?

2.24 Quality Management Plan: Customer Information Control System

495. No superfluous information or marketing narrative?

496. How are calibration records kept?

497. Was trending evident between reviews?

498. Is the steering committee active in Customer Information Control System project oversight?

499. What else should you do now?

500. Is this process still needed?

501. How does your organization determine the requirements and product/service features important to customers?

502. How does training support what is important to your organization and the individual?

503. Does the program conduct field testing?

504. How do your action plans support the strategic objectives?

505. Are qmps good forever?

506. What is the return on investment?

507. How are new requirements or changes to requirements identified?

508. Written by multiple authors and in multiple writing styles?

509. What does it do for you (or to me)?

510. Show/provide copy of procedures for taking field notes?

511. How do you measure?

512. Is there a Quality Management Plan?

513. Does the program use modeling in the permitting or decision-making processes?

2.25 Quality Metrics: Customer Information Control System

514. What documentation is required?

515. Which are the right metrics to use?

516. Product Availability ?

517. Is the reporting frequency appropriate?

518. Filter visualizations of interest?

519. What happens if you get an abnormal result?

520. How do you communicate results and findings to upper management?

521. The metrics–what is being considered?

522. What percentage are outcome-based?

523. Has trace of defects been initiated?

524. What group is empowered to define quality requirements?

525. Does risk analysis documentation meet standards?

526. Was the overall quality better or worse than previous products?

527. Should a modifier be included?

528. How exactly do you define when differences exist?

529. Are documents on hand to provide explanations of privacy and confidentiality?

530. Where is quality now?

531. Are quality metrics defined?

532. Have risk areas been identified?

2.26 Process Improvement Plan: Customer Information Control System

533. To elicit goal statements, do you ask a question such as, What do you want to achieve?

534. Does explicit definition of the measures exist?

535. What personnel are the champions for the initiative?

536. Are you making progress on the improvement framework?

537. Everyone agrees on what process improvement is, right?

538. Are you making progress on your improvement plan?

539. Have the supporting tools been developed or acquired?

540. Does your process ensure quality?

541. Are there forms and procedures to collect and record the data?

542. What personnel are the coaches for your initiative?

543. What is the test-cycle concept?

544. Where do you want to be?

545. Have storage and access mechanisms and procedures been determined?

546. Are you following the quality standards?

547. Are you meeting the quality standards?

548. If a process improvement framework is being used, which elements will help the problems and goals listed?

549. Has a process guide to collect the data been developed?

550. Why quality management?

551. What personnel are the change agents for your initiative?

2.27 Responsibility Assignment Matrix: Customer Information Control System

552. Does the Customer Information Control System project need to be analyzed further to uncover additional responsibilities?

553. Contemplated overhead expenditure for each period based on the best information currently available?

554. Who is the Customer Information Control System project Manager?

555. What is the justification?

556. Are the requirements for all items of overhead established by rational, traceable processes?

557. The staff interests – is the group or the person interested in working for this Customer Information Control System project?

558. Not any rs, as, or cs: if an identified role is only informed, should others be eliminated from the matrix?

559. What are the known stakeholder requirements?

560. Changes in the direct base to which overhead costs are allocated?

561. Authorization to proceed with all authorized work?

562. Incurrence of actual indirect costs in excess of budgets, by element of expense?

563. Is the anticipated (firm and potential) business base Customer Information Control System projected in a rational, consistent manner?

564. Evaluate the impact of schedule changes, work around, etc?

565. Do work packages consist of discrete tasks which are adequately described?

566. Are indirect costs accumulated for comparison with the corresponding budgets?

567. Does the contractors system provide unit or lot costs when applicable?

568. Are people afraid to let you know when others are under allocated?

569. Direct labor dollars and/or hours?

2.28 Roles and Responsibilities: Customer Information Control System

570. What is working well?

571. Is feedback clearly communicated and non-judgmental?

572. What is working well within your organizations performance management system?

573. What should you highlight for improvement?

574. Concern: where are you limited or have no authority, where you can not influence?

575. What expectations were NOT met?

576. Who is responsible for implementation activities and where will the functions, roles and responsibilities be defined?

577. Are the quality assurance functions and related roles and responsibilities clearly defined?

578. Is the data complete?

579. What areas would you highlight for changes or improvements?

580. Is there a training program in place for stakeholders covering expectations, roles and responsibilities and any addition knowledge others

need to be good stakeholders?

581. What are your major roles and responsibilities in the area of performance measurement and assessment?

582. Are Customer Information Control System project team roles and responsibilities identified and documented?

583. Attainable / achievable: the goal is attainable; can you actually accomplish the goal?

584. Are your policies supportive of a culture of quality data?

585. What should you do now to ensure that you are exceeding expectations and excelling in your current position?

586. Be specific; avoid generalities. Thank you and great work alone are insufficient. What exactly do you appreciate and why?

587. What should you do now to prepare yourself for a promotion, increased responsibilities or a different job?

2.29 Human Resource Management Plan: Customer Information Control System

588. Does the business case include how the Customer Information Control System project aligns with your organizations strategic goals & objectives?

589. Have the key functions and capabilities been defined and assigned to each release or iteration?

590. Have Customer Information Control System project success criteria been defined?

591. Timeline and milestones?

592. Have the key elements of a coherent Customer Information Control System project management strategy been established?

593. Is your organization heading towards expansion, outsourcing of certain talents or making cut-backs to save money?

594. Are all payments made according to the contract(s)?

595. Are meeting minutes captured and sent out after the meeting?

596. Are Customer Information Control System project contact logs kept up to date?

597. Is there an approved case?

598. Are risk triggers captured?

599. Have reserves been created to address risks?

600. Where is your organization headed?

601. Are all vendor contracts closed out?

602. Are action items captured and managed?

603. Is a pmo (Customer Information Control System project management office) in place and provide oversight to the Customer Information Control System project?

604. Are all resource assumptions documented?

605. Is your organization human?

606. Is the steering committee active in Customer Information Control System project oversight?

2.30 Communications Management Plan: Customer Information Control System

607. What approaches do you use?

608. What data is going to be required?

609. Is the stakeholder role recognized by your organization?

610. What is Customer Information Control System project communications management?

611. What are the interrelationships?

612. What is the political influence?

613. Who will use or be affected by the result of a Customer Information Control System project?

614. What steps can you take for a positive relationship?

615. Timing: when do the effects of the communication take place?

616. Who is responsible?

617. Who is involved as you identify stakeholders?

618. Who needs to know and how much?

619. What approaches to you feel are the best ones to use?

620. Who did you turn to if you had questions?

621. In your work, how much time is spent on stakeholder identification?

622. Who are the members of the governing body?

623. Do you ask; can you recommend others for you to talk with about this initiative?

624. Which stakeholders are thought leaders, influences, or early adopters?

625. Are you constantly rushing from meeting to meeting?

2.31 Risk Management Plan: Customer Information Control System

626. Do requirements demand the use of new analysis, design, or testing methods?

627. Can the Customer Information Control System project proceed without assuming the risk?

628. Is Customer Information Control System project scope stable?

629. Can you stabilize dynamic risk factors?

630. Degree of confidence in estimated size estimate?

631. Are Customer Information Control System project requirements stable?

632. For software; does the software interface with new or unproven hardware or unproven vendor products?

633. Are end-users enthusiastically committed to the Customer Information Control System project and the system/product to be built?

634. Is the customer willing to establish rapid communication links with the developer?

635. Have staff received necessary training?

636. Is the customer willing to participate in reviews?

637. How risk averse are you?

638. Does the Customer Information Control System project team have experience with the technology to be implemented?

639. How well were you able to manage your risk before?

640. Are formal technical reviews part of this process?

641. Which is an input to the risk management process?

642. What are the chances the event will occur?

643. What things are likely to change?

2.32 Risk Register: Customer Information Control System

644. Does the evidence highlight any areas to advance opportunities or foster good relations. If yes what steps will be taken?

645. Contingency actions - planned actions to reduce the immediate seriousness of the risk when it does occur. What should you do when?

646. Why would you develop a risk register?

647. What should you do when?

648. Are there other alternative controls that could be implemented?

649. Methodology: how will risk management be performed on this Customer Information Control System project?

650. What are the main aims, objectives of the policy, strategy, or service and the intended outcomes?

651. Risk categories: what are the main categories of risks that should be addressed on this Customer Information Control System project?

652. Which key risks have ineffective responses or outstanding improvement actions?

653. What is the probability and impact of the risk

occurring?

654. What is the reason for current performance gaps and do the risks and opportunities identified previously account for this?

655. Assume the risk event or situation happens, what would the impact be?

656. Is further information required before making a decision?

657. Schedule impact/severity estimated range (workdays) assume the event happens, what is the potential impact?

658. Have other controls and solutions been implemented in other services which could be applied as an alternative to additional funding?

659. What could prevent you delivering on the strategic program objectives and what is being done to mitigate corresponding issues?

660. Are your objectives at risk?

661. Are corrective measures implemented as planned?

2.33 Probability and Impact Assessment: Customer Information Control System

662. Does the customer have a solid idea of what is required?

663. What are the preparations required for facing difficulties?

664. Risk urgency assessment -which of your risks could occur soon, or require a longer planning time?

665. Are there alternative opinions/solutions/ processes you should explore?

666. How much is the probability of a risk occurring?

667. What are the chances the risk event will occur?

668. What is the likelihood of a breakthrough?

669. What new technologies are being explored in the same area?

670. What are its business ethics?

671. Are there new risks that mitigation strategies might introduce?

672. Assumptions analysis -what assumptions have you made or been given about your Customer Information Control System project?

673. What will be the environmental impact of the Customer Information Control System project?

674. Do you use any methods to analyze risks?

675. Should the risk be taken at all?

676. Do you train all developers in the process?

677. Which role do you have in the Customer Information Control System project?

678. Are the best people available?

679. Workarounds are determined during which step of risk management?

680. How is the Customer Information Control System project going to be managed?

681. Risk may be made during which step of risk management?

2.34 Probability and Impact Matrix: Customer Information Control System

682. What will be the impact or consequence if the risk occurs?

683. Are staff committed for the duration of the Customer Information Control System project?

684. Which phase of the Customer Information Control System project do you take part in?

685. Who has experience with this?

686. What is the likelihood?

687. Could others have been better mitigated?

688. Why do you need to manage Customer Information Control System project Risk?

689. Who is going to be the consortium leader?

690. During which risk management process is a determination to transfer a risk made?

691. Are tool mentors available?

692. What are the likely future requirements?

693. What things might go wrong?

694. What will be the environmental impact of the

Customer Information Control System project?

695. How will the consumption pattern change?

696. How well were you able to manage your risk?

697. What can you use the analyzed risks for?

698. Do you need a risk management plan?

699. Do others match with the clients requirement?

2.35 Risk Data Sheet: Customer Information Control System

700. What are the main threats to your existence?

701. Potential for recurrence?

702. Who has a vested interest in how you perform as your organization (our stakeholders)?

703. What was measured?

704. What will be the consequences if the risk happens?

705. If it happens, what are the consequences?

706. What do people affected think about the need for, and practicality of preventive measures?

707. What were the Causes that contributed?

708. During work activities could hazards exist?

709. What if client refuses?

710. What are you weak at and therefore need to do better?

711. Has a sensitivity analysis been carried out?

712. What are your core values?

713. Whom do you serve (customers)?

714. What is the likelihood of it happening?

715. How can hazards be reduced?

716. What actions can be taken to eliminate or remove risk?

717. Do effective diagnostic tests exist?

2.36 Procurement Management Plan: Customer Information Control System

718. Are internal Customer Information Control System project status meetings held at reasonable intervals?

719. Are Customer Information Control System project team members committed fulltime?

720. Are enough systems & user personnel assigned to the Customer Information Control System project?

721. Were Customer Information Control System project team members involved in detailed estimating and scheduling?

722. What types of contracts will be used?

723. Are quality inspections and review activities listed in the Customer Information Control System project schedule(s)?

724. Financial capacity; does the seller have, or can the seller reasonably be expected to obtain, the financial resources needed?

725. Are the Customer Information Control System project team members located locally to the users/stakeholders?

726. If independent estimates will be needed as evaluation criteria, who will prepare them and when?

727. Are milestone deliverables effectively tracked and compared to Customer Information Control System project plan?

728. Are cause and effect determined for risks when others occur?

729. What are things that you need to improve?

730. Are the results of quality assurance reviews provided to affected groups & individuals?

731. Has the scope management document been updated and distributed to help prevent scope creep?

732. Is there an on-going process in place to monitor Customer Information Control System project risks?

733. Are the schedule estimates reasonable given the Customer Information Control System project?

734. What are your quality assurance overheads?

735. Are the payment terms being followed?

2.37 Source Selection Criteria: Customer Information Control System

736. How do you ensure an integrated assessment of proposals?

737. If the costs are normalized, please account for how the normalization is conducted. Is a cost realism analysis used?

738. How should comments received in response to a RFP be handled?

739. How can business terms and conditions be improved to yield more effective price competition?

740. When and what information can be considered with offerors regarding past performance?

741. How should the oral presentations be handled?

742. What are the special considerations for preaward debriefings?

743. How should the preproposal conference be conducted?

744. When should debriefings be held and how should they be scheduled?

745. What are open book debriefings?

746. How can the methods of publicizing the buy be

tailored to yield more effective price competition?

747. What can not be disclosed?

748. What procedures are followed when a contractor requires access to classified information or a significant quantity of special material/information?

749. Is a letter of commitment from each proposed team member and key subcontractor included?

750. How do you facilitate evaluation against published criteria?

751. What is cost analysis and when should it be performed?

752. What documentation should be used to support the selection decision?

753. Are they compliant with all technical requirements?

754. Are there any common areas of weaknesses or deficiencies in the proposals in the competitive range?

755. Do proposed hours support content and schedule?

2.38 Stakeholder Management Plan: Customer Information Control System

756. Is documentation created for communication with the suppliers and vendors?

757. Describe the process that will be used to design, develop, review, accept, distribute and change outputs. Will all outputs delivered by the Customer Information Control System project follow the same process?

758. Where are the verification requirements to be documented (eg purchase order, agreement etc)?

759. Has a Customer Information Control System project Communications Plan been developed?

760. Where to get additional help?

761. Quality assurance overheads?

762. What are the criteria for selecting other suppliers, including subcontractors?

763. What conditions make using three-point estimating justifiable?

764. Are Customer Information Control System project contact logs kept up to date?

765. Were the budget estimates reasonable?

766. Alignment to strategic goals & objectives?

767. Are requirements management tracking tools and procedures in place?

768. What is the drawback in using qualitative Customer Information Control System project selection techniques?

769. What specific resources will be required for implementation activities?

770. Is staff trained on the software technologies that are being used on the Customer Information Control System project?

771. Has a structured approach been used to break work effort into manageable components (WBS)?

772. Is the steering committee active in Customer Information Control System project oversight?

2.39 Change Management Plan: Customer Information Control System

773. Who will fund the training?

774. What relationships will change?

775. Clearly articulate the overall business benefits of the Customer Information Control System project -why are you doing this now?

776. Would you need to tailor a special message for each segment of the audience?

777. Impact of systems implementation on organization change?

778. Who should be involved in developing a change management strategy?

779. How does the principle of senders and receivers make the Customer Information Control System project communications effort more complex?

780. What is going to be done differently?

781. Will all field readiness criteria have been practically met prior to training roll-out?

782. Has an information & communications plan been developed?

783. Who in the business it includes?

784. What new competencies will be required for the roles?

785. What is the worst thing that can happen if you chose not to communicate this information?

786. Has the target training audience been identified and nominated?

787. Has the priority for this Customer Information Control System project been set by the Business Unit Management Team?

788. Who will do the training?

789. Where will the funds come from?

790. Readiness -what is a successful end state?

3.0 Executing Process Group: Customer Information Control System

791. What are the critical steps involved with strategy mapping?

792. What are the Customer Information Control System project management deliverables of each process group?

793. Do the products created live up to the necessary quality?

794. Do the partners have sufficient financial capacity to keep up the benefits produced by the programme?

795. What are crucial elements of successful Customer Information Control System project plan execution?

796. Does the Customer Information Control System project team have the right skills?

797. Are escalated issues resolved promptly?

798. Who will be the main sponsor?

799. How could stakeholders negatively impact your Customer Information Control System project?

800. How do you control progress of your Customer Information Control System project?

801. What were things that you did very well and

want to do the same again on the next Customer Information Control System project?

802. Will outside resources be needed to help?

803. How does the job market and current state of the economy affect human resource management?

804. Do your results resemble a normal distribution?

805. Is activity definition the first process involved in Customer Information Control System project time management?

806. How will you avoid scope creep?

807. If action is called for, what form should it take?

808. How does a Customer Information Control System project life cycle differ from a product life cycle?

3.1 Team Member Status Report: Customer Information Control System

809. Will the staff do training or is that done by a third party?

810. Why is it to be done?

811. Do you have an Enterprise Customer Information Control System project Management Office (EPMO)?

812. What specific interest groups do you have in place?

813. How does this product, good, or service meet the needs of the Customer Information Control System project and your organization as a whole?

814. Are the products of your organizations Customer Information Control System projects meeting customers objectives?

815. How it is to be done?

816. Does the product, good, or service already exist within your organization?

817. How much risk is involved?

818. The problem with Reward & Recognition Programs is that the truly deserving people all too often get left out. How can you make it practical?

819. Are your organizations Customer Information Control System projects more successful over time?

820. When a teams productivity and success depend on collaboration and the efficient flow of information, what generally fails them?

821. How will resource planning be done?

822. Does your organization have the means (staff, money, contract, etc.) to produce or to acquire the product, good, or service?

823. How can you make it practical?

824. Are the attitudes of staff regarding Customer Information Control System project work improving?

825. Does every department have to have a Customer Information Control System project Manager on staff?

826. Is there evidence that staff is taking a more professional approach toward management of your organizations Customer Information Control System projects?

827. What is to be done?

3.2 Change Request: Customer Information Control System

828. How do team members communicate with each other?

829. How can changes be graded?

830. What needs to be communicated?

831. Are you implementing itil processes?

832. How do you get changes (code) out in a timely manner?

833. What are the duties of the change control team?

834. Are change requests logged and managed?

835. What should be regulated in a change control operating instruction?

836. Screen shots or attachments included in a Change Request?

837. Who will perform the change?

838. Have scm procedures for noting the change, recording it, and reporting it been followed?

839. What are the basic mechanics of the Change Advisory Board (CAB)?

840. What has an inspector to inspect and to check?

841. Has a formal technical review been conducted to assess technical correctness?

842. Will the change use memory to the extent that other functions will be not have sufficient memory to operate effectively?

843. Who can suggest changes?

844. Who is responsible for the implementation and monitoring of all measures?

845. What is the purpose of change control?

846. What type of changes does change control take into account?

847. Can you answer what happened, who did it, when did it happen, and what else will be affected?

3.3 Change Log: Customer Information Control System

848. Is the change request open, closed or pending?

849. Is the requested change request a result of changes in other Customer Information Control System project(s)?

850. Is the submitted change a new change or a modification of a previously approved change?

851. Who initiated the change request?

852. When was the request submitted?

853. How does this relate to the standards developed for specific business processes?

854. How does this change affect the timeline of the schedule?

855. Does the suggested change request represent a desired enhancement to the products functionality?

856. Is this a mandatory replacement?

857. Does the suggested change request seem to represent a necessary enhancement to the product?

858. Will the Customer Information Control System project fail if the change request is not executed?

859. How does this change affect scope?

860. Is the change backward compatible without limitations?

861. Is the change request within Customer Information Control System project scope?

862. Where do changes come from?

863. When was the request approved?

864. Do the described changes impact on the integrity or security of the system?

3.4 Decision Log: Customer Information Control System

865. How effective is maintaining the log at facilitating organizational learning?

866. It becomes critical to track and periodically revisit both operational effectiveness; Are you noticing all that you need to, and are you interpreting what you see effectively?

867. Who will be given a copy of this document and where will it be kept?

868. Does anything need to be adjusted?

869. What alternatives/risks were considered?

870. Is everything working as expected?

871. How does provision of information, both in terms of content and presentation, influence acceptance of alternative strategies?

872. How do you know when you are achieving it?

873. Decision-making process; how will the team make decisions?

874. What makes you different or better than others companies selling the same thing?

875. What is the line where eDiscovery ends and

document review begins?

876. With whom was the decision shared or considered?

877. Who is the decisionmaker?

878. How does an increasing emphasis on cost containment influence the strategies and tactics used?

879. Linked to original objective?

880. What was the rationale for the decision?

881. Which variables make a critical difference?

882. Is your opponent open to a non-traditional workflow, or will it likely challenge anything you do?

883. How do you define success?

884. Meeting purpose; why does this team meet?

3.5 Quality Audit: Customer Information Control System

885. How does your organization know that its general support services planning and management systems are appropriately effective and constructive?

886. Are storage areas and reconditioning operations designed to prevent mix-ups and assure orderly handling of both the distressed and reconditioned devices?

887. Is your organizational structure a help or a hindrance to deployment?

888. How does your organization know that its staff support services planning and management systems are appropriately effective and constructive?

889. How does your organization know whether they are adhering to mission and achieving objectives?

890. How does your organization know that its security arrangements are appropriately effective and constructive?

891. How does your organization know that its staffing profile is optimally aligned with the capability requirements implicit (or explicit) in its Strategic Plan?

892. How well do you think your organization engages with the outside community?

893. How does your organization know that its system for inducting new staff to maximize workplace contributions are appropriately effective and constructive?

894. How does your organization know that its planning processes are appropriately effective and constructive?

895. Is there a written corporate quality policy?

896. How does your organization know that its system for examining work done is appropriately effective and constructive?

897. Are multiple statements on the same issue consistent with each other?

898. Are there sufficient personnel having the necessary education, background, training, and experience to assure that all operations are correctly performed?

899. What are you trying to accomplish with this audit?

900. What will the Observer get to Observe?

901. How does your organization know that its management system is appropriately effective and constructive?

902. What experience do staff have in the type of work that the audit entails?

903. How does your organization know that its

systems for providing high quality consultancy services to external parties are appropriately effective and constructive?

904. Can your organization demonstrate exactly how and why results were achieved?

3.6 Team Directory: Customer Information Control System

905. Days from the time the issue is identified?

906. Who are the Team Members?

907. When does information need to be distributed?

908. Timing: when do the effects of communication take place?

909. Who will be the stakeholders on your next Customer Information Control System project?

910. Who is the Sponsor?

911. Who are your stakeholders (customers, sponsors, end users, team members)?

912. Process decisions: are contractors adequately prosecuting the work?

913. Process decisions: are there any statutory or regulatory issues relevant to the timely execution of work?

914. What are you going to deliver or accomplish?

915. Who will talk to the customer?

916. Process decisions: how well was task order work performed?

917. Decisions: is the most suitable form of contract being used?

918. How do unidentified risks impact the outcome of the Customer Information Control System project?

919. Process decisions: do invoice amounts match accepted work in place?

920. Decisions: what could be done better to improve the quality of the constructed product?

921. Process decisions: are all start-up, turn over and close out requirements of the contract satisfied?

922. How will you accomplish and manage the objectives?

923. Who should receive information (all stakeholders)?

3.7 Team Operating Agreement: Customer Information Control System

924. Seconds for members to respond?

925. Methodologies: how will key team processes be implemented, such as training, research, work deliverable production, review and approval processes, knowledge management, and meeting procedures?

926. Do you leverage technology engagement tools group chat, polls, screen sharing, etc.?

927. Are there more than two national cultures represented by your team?

928. Must your team members rely on the expertise of other members to complete tasks?

929. Have you set the goals and objectives of the team?

930. Does your team need access to all documents and information at all times?

931. How does teaming fit in with overall organizational goals and meet organizational needs?

932. Why does your organization want to participate in teaming?

933. Do you ensure that all participants know how to

use the required technology?

934. Do you listen for voice tone and word choice to understand the meaning behind words?

935. Do you vary your voice pace, tone and pitch to engage participants and gain involvement?

936. Are there more than two functional areas represented by your team?

937. Do team members reside in more than two countries?

938. What are the boundaries (organizational or geographic) within which you operate?

939. Do you call or email participants to ensure understanding, follow-through and commitment to the meeting outcomes?

940. What types of accommodations will be formulated and put in place for sustaining the team?

941. What administrative supports will be put in place to support the team and the teams supervisor?

942. Confidentiality: how will confidential information be handled?

943. What individual strengths does each team member bring to the group?

3.8 Team Performance Assessment: Customer Information Control System

944. How does Customer Information Control System project termination impact Customer Information Control System project team members?

945. What structural changes have you made or are you preparing to make?

946. What are you doing specifically to develop the leaders around you?

947. To what degree can the team measure progress against specific goals?

948. Do friends perform better than acquaintances?

949. Is there a particular method of data analysis that you would recommend as a means of demonstrating that method variance is not of great concern for a given dataset?

950. To what degree does the team possess adequate membership to achieve its ends?

951. To what degree will new and supplemental skills be introduced as the need is recognized?

952. To what degree does the teams work approach provide opportunity for members to engage in open interaction?

953. To what degree will the team adopt a concrete, clearly understood, and agreed-upon approach that will result in achievement of the teams goals?

954. To what degree are the members clear on what they are individually responsible for and what they are jointly responsible for?

955. To what degree are the goals ambitious?

956. Delaying market entry: how long is too long?

957. To what degree are staff involved as partners in the improvement process?

958. To what degree will team members, individually and collectively, commit time to help themselves and others learn and develop skills?

959. To what degree will the team ensure that all members equitably share the work essential to the success of the team?

960. To what degree are corresponding categories of skills either actually or potentially represented across the membership?

961. To what degree can team members meet frequently enough to accomplish the teams ends?

962. How do you encourage members to learn from each other?

963. To what degree do members understand and articulate the same purpose without relying on ambiguous abstractions?

3.9 Team Member Performance Assessment: Customer Information Control System

964. How should adaptive assessments be implemented?

965. What is collaboration?

966. How do you make use of research?

967. In what areas would you like to concentrate your knowledge and resources?

968. To what degree are the relative importance and priority of the goals clear to all team members?

969. What evaluation results did you have?

970. How is assessment information achieved, stored?

971. To what degree are the teams goals and objectives clear, simple, and measurable?

972. What future plans (e.g., modifications) do you have for your program?

973. What makes them effective?

974. How is the timing of assessments organized (e.g., pre/post-test, single point during training, multiple reassessment during training)?

975. How accurately is your plan implemented?

976. Should a ratee get a copy of all the raters documents about the employees performance?

977. Are the goals SMART ?

978. What evaluation results do you have?

979. What, if any, steps are available for employees who feel they have been unfairly or inaccurately rated?

980. To what degree do all members feel responsible for all agreed-upon measures?

981. Does adaptive training work?

982. What is the Business Management Oversight Process?

3.10 Issue Log: Customer Information Control System

983. How do you manage human resources?

984. Why not more evaluators?

985. Which team member will work with each stakeholder?

986. Who have you worked with in past, similar initiatives?

987. Where do team members get information?

988. How do you manage communications?

989. Why multiple evaluators?

990. Are there potential barriers between the team and the stakeholder?

991. Who is the stakeholder?

992. Are the Customer Information Control System project issues uniquely identified, including to which product they refer?

993. What is the stakeholders political influence?

994. Is the issue log kept in a safe place?

995. What is the status of the issue?

996. What effort will a change need?

997. Are they needed?

998. How much time does it take to do it?

999. Who reported the issue?

4.0 Monitoring and Controlling Process Group: Customer Information Control System

1000. Are the necessary foundations in place to ensure the sustainability of the results of the programme?

1001. How were collaborations developed, and how are they sustained?

1002. What areas does the group agree are the biggest success on the Customer Information Control System project?

1003. Overall, how does the program function to serve the clients?

1004. How is agile portfolio management done?

1005. What were things that you did very well and want to do the same again on the next Customer Information Control System project?

1006. Is the program making progress in helping to achieve the set results?

1007. How well defined and documented were the Customer Information Control System project management processes you chose to use?

1008. Just how important is your work to the overall success of the Customer Information Control System project?

1009. What resources (both financial and non-financial) are available/needed?

1010. What areas were overlooked on this Customer Information Control System project?

1011. Did the Customer Information Control System project team have enough people to execute the Customer Information Control System project plan?

1012. Is progress on outcomes due to your program?

1013. Is the program in place as intended?

1014. How is Agile Customer Information Control System project Management done?

1015. How are you doing?

1016. What resources are necessary?

4.1 Project Performance Report: Customer Information Control System

1017. To what degree can the team ensure that all members are individually and jointly accountable for the teams purpose, goals, approach, and work-products?

1018. To what degree are the goals realistic?

1019. What is the degree to which rules govern information exchange between groups?

1020. To what degree will each member have the opportunity to advance his or her professional skills in all three of the above categories while contributing to the accomplishment of the teams purpose and goals?

1021. To what degree does the information network communicate information relevant to the task?

1022. To what degree is the information network consistent with the structure of the formal organization?

1023. To what degree do team members feel that the purpose of the team is important, if not exciting?

1024. To what degree do team members agree with the goals, relative importance, and the ways in which achievement will be measured?

1025. What degree are the relative importance and

priority of the goals clear to all team members?

1026. To what degree does the information network provide individuals with the information they require?

1027. To what degree does the informal organization make use of individual resources and meet individual needs?

1028. To what degree do team members frequently explore the teams purpose and its implications?

1029. To what degree do team members articulate the teams work approach?

1030. To what degree are the skill areas critical to team performance present?

1031. To what degree are the structures of the formal organization consistent with the behaviors in the informal organization?

1032. To what degree is there centralized control of information sharing?

4.2 Variance Analysis: Customer Information Control System

1033. What is the actual cost of work performed?

1034. Are significant decision points, constraints, and interfaces identified as key milestones?

1035. What is the total budget for the Customer Information Control System project (including estimates for authorized and unpriced work)?

1036. Historical experience?

1037. Are all authorized tasks assigned to identified organizational elements?

1038. How do you manage changes in the nature of the overhead requirements?

1039. Are there changes in the direct base to which overhead costs are allocated?

1040. How are material, labor, and overhead standards set?

1041. What is the dollar amount of the fluctuation?

1042. What business event causes fluctuations?

1043. How does your organization allocate the cost of shared expenses and services?

1044. What is the performance to date and material commitment?

1045. What should management do?

1046. Are overhead costs budgets established on a basis consistent with the anticipated direct business base?

1047. Are estimates of costs at completion generated in a rational, consistent manner?

1048. Contemplated overhead expenditure for each period based on the best information currently is available?

1049. How have the setting and use of standards changed over time?

1050. There are detailed schedules which support control account and work package start and completion dates/events?

1051. Are overhead cost budgets established for each department which has authority to incur overhead costs?

4.3 Earned Value Status: Customer Information Control System

1052. Are you hitting your Customer Information Control System projects targets?

1053. If earned value management (EVM) is so good in determining the true status of a Customer Information Control System project and Customer Information Control System project its completion, why is it that hardly any one uses it in information systems related Customer Information Control System projects?

1054. Earned value can be used in almost any Customer Information Control System project situation and in almost any Customer Information Control System project environment. it may be used on large Customer Information Control System projects, medium sized Customer Information Control System projects, tiny Customer Information Control System projects (in cut-down form), complex and simple Customer Information Control System projects and in any market sector. some people, of course, know all about earned value, they have used it for years - but perhaps not as effectively as they could have?

1055. How much is it going to cost by the finish?

1056. Verification is a process of ensuring that the developed system satisfies the stakeholders agreements and specifications; Are you building the product right? What do you verify?

1057. What is the unit of forecast value?

1058. Validation is a process of ensuring that the developed system will actually achieve the stakeholders desired outcomes; Are you building the right product? What do you validate?

1059. Where are your problem areas?

1060. How does this compare with other Customer Information Control System projects?

1061. Where is evidence-based earned value in your organization reported?

1062. When is it going to finish?

4.4 Risk Audit: Customer Information Control System

1063. Does your auditor understand your business?

1064. Do all coaches/instructors/leaders have appropriate and current accreditation?

1065. Are auditors able to effectively apply more soft evidence found in the risk-assessment process with the results of more tangible audit evidence found through more substantive testing?

1066. Are team members trained in the use of the tools?

1067. What risk does not having unique identification present?

1068. Is risk an management agenda item?

1069. Are procedures in place to ensure the security of staff and information and compliance with privacy legislation if applicable?

1070. Is your organization able to present documentary evidence in support of compliance?

1071. What limitations do auditors face in effectively applying risk-assessment results to the risk of material misstatement measures?

1072. Is safety information provided to all involved?

1073. Do you have an emergency plan?

1074. Does your organization communicate regularly and effectively with its members?

1075. Do you record and file all audits?

1076. Is there a clear procedure for reporting accidents/injuries?

1077. Are you meeting your legal, regulatory and compliance requirements - if not, why not?

1078. Are requirements fully understood by the team and customers?

1079. Is your organization willing to commit significant time to the requirements gathering process?

1080. Is the auditor truly independent?

1081. Have reasonable steps been taken to reduce the risks to acceptable levels?

1082. What is the implication of budget constraint on this process?

4.5 Contractor Status Report: Customer Information Control System

1083. Describe how often regular updates are made to the proposed solution. Are corresponding regular updates included in the standard maintenance plan?

1084. What is the average response time for answering a support call?

1085. How is risk transferred?

1086. What was the budget or estimated cost for your organizations services?

1087. How long have you been using the services?

1088. How does the proposed individual meet each requirement?

1089. Who can list a Customer Information Control System project as organization experience, your organization or a previous employee of your organization?

1090. What process manages the contracts?

1091. Are there contractual transfer concerns?

1092. What was the actual budget or estimated cost for your organizations services?

1093. If applicable; describe your standard schedule

for new software version releases. Are new software version releases included in the standard maintenance plan?

1094. What was the overall budget or estimated cost?

1095. What are the minimum and optimal bandwidth requirements for the proposed solution?

1096. What was the final actual cost?

4.6 Formal Acceptance: Customer Information Control System

1097. Do you buy pre-configured systems or build your own configuration?

1098. Was the Customer Information Control System project work done on time, within budget, and according to specification?

1099. General estimate of the costs and times to complete the Customer Information Control System project?

1100. Was the Customer Information Control System project managed well?

1101. Do you perform formal acceptance or burn-in tests?

1102. Was business value realized?

1103. How does your team plan to obtain formal acceptance on your Customer Information Control System project?

1104. Do you buy-in installation services?

1105. What can you do better next time?

1106. How well did the team follow the methodology?

1107. Who would use it?

1108. Is formal acceptance of the Customer Information Control System project product documented and distributed?

1109. Was the Customer Information Control System project goal achieved?

1110. Did the Customer Information Control System project achieve its MOV?

1111. Who supplies data?

1112. Was the sponsor/customer satisfied?

1113. Does it do what Customer Information Control System project team said it would?

1114. What are the requirements against which to test, Who will execute?

1115. What lessons were learned about your Customer Information Control System project management methodology?

1116. What was done right?

5.0 Closing Process Group: Customer Information Control System

1117. What areas does the group agree are the biggest success on the Customer Information Control System project?

1118. Based on your Customer Information Control System project communication management plan, what worked well?

1119. Was the user/client satisfied with the end product?

1120. How critical is the Customer Information Control System project success to the success of your organization?

1121. What can you do better next time, and what specific actions can you take to improve?

1122. Can the lesson learned be replicated?

1123. What were things that you did very well and want to do the same again on the next Customer Information Control System project?

1124. Did the delivered product meet the specified requirements and goals of the Customer Information Control System project?

1125. Does the close educate others to improve performance?

1126. What is the Customer Information Control System project name and date of completion?

1127. What was learned?

1128. Were risks identified and mitigated?

1129. Was the schedule met?

1130. What is an Encumbrance?

1131. If a risk event occurs, what will you do?

1132. What could have been improved?

1133. Will the Customer Information Control System project deliverable(s) replace a current asset or group of assets?

5.1 Procurement Audit: Customer Information Control System

1134. Were any additional works or deliveries admissible without the need for a new procurement procedure?

1135. Are there procedures for trade-in arrangements?

1136. Did the contracting authority draw up a comprehensive written report about progress and outcome of the procurement process?

1137. Budget controls: does your organization maintain an up-to-date (approved) budget for all funded activities, and perform a comparison of that budget with actual expenditures for each budget category?

1138. How are you making the audit trail easy to follow?

1139. Does the procurement function/unit have the ability to negotiate with customers and suppliers?

1140. Are reports based on sound data available to the already stated responsible for monitoring the performance of contracts?

1141. Did the additional works introduce minor or non-substantial changes to performance, as described in the contract documents?

1142. Does the procurement unit have sound commercial awareness and knowledge of suppliers and the market?

1143. Has management taken the necessary steps to ensure that relevant control systems are always up to date?

1144. Is it on a regular basis examined whether it is possible to enter into public private partnerships with private suppliers?

1145. Are there procedures to ensure that changes to purchase orders will be updated on the computer files?

1146. Are lease-purchase agreements drawn and processed in accordance with law and regulation?

1147. Is the procurement process organized the most appropriate way taking into consideration the amount of procurement?

1148. Is the foreseen budget compared with similar Customer Information Control System projects or procurements yet realised (historical standards)?

1149. Were additional works strictly necessary for the completion of performance under the contract?

1150. Which are the main risks and controls of each phase?

1151. Is there no evidence of favouritism towards a particular contractor during the evaluation and negotiation processes?

1152. Does your organization have an administrative timetable to assist the staff in implementing the budget calendar?

1153. Which are main risks and controls of each phase?

5.2 Contract Close-Out: Customer Information Control System

1154. Have all acceptance criteria been met prior to final payment to contractors?

1155. Have all contracts been completed?

1156. Why Outsource?

1157. Was the contract type appropriate?

1158. Have all contract records been included in the Customer Information Control System project archives?

1159. Are the signers the authorized officials?

1160. How/when used ?

1161. How is the contracting office notified of the automatic contract close-out?

1162. Parties: who is involved?

1163. Parties: Authorized?

1164. Have all contracts been closed?

1165. Change in knowledge?

1166. Change in circumstances?

1167. What is capture management?

1168. Has each contract been audited to verify acceptance and delivery?

1169. Was the contract sufficiently clear so as not to result in numerous disputes and misunderstandings?

1170. Was the contract complete without requiring numerous changes and revisions?

1171. Change in attitude or behavior?

1172. What happens to the recipient of services?

1173. How does it work?

5.3 Project or Phase Close-Out: Customer Information Control System

1174. What are the marketing communication needs for each stakeholder?

1175. What is this stakeholder expecting?

1176. Planned completion date?

1177. Did the Customer Information Control System project management methodology work?

1178. What was expected from each stakeholder?

1179. In addition to assessing whether the Customer Information Control System project was successful, it is equally critical to analyze why it was or was not fully successful. Are you including this?

1180. What information is each stakeholder group interested in?

1181. Which changes might a stakeholder be required to make as a result of the Customer Information Control System project?

1182. Planned remaining costs?

1183. What hierarchical authority does the stakeholder have in your organization?

1184. What information did each stakeholder need

to contribute to the Customer Information Control System projects success?

1185. What is a Risk Management Process?

1186. What was the preferred delivery mechanism?

1187. Who controlled the resources for the Customer Information Control System project?

1188. What process was planned for managing issues/risks?

1189. Who is responsible for award close-out?

1190. Is the lesson significant, valid, and applicable?

1191. Is there a clear cause and effect between the activity and the lesson learned?

5.4 Lessons Learned: Customer Information Control System

1192. How effective was the documentation that you received with the Customer Information Control System project product/service?

1193. What did you put in place to ensure success?

1194. What data are likely to be missing?

1195. How was the quality of products/processes assured?

1196. What needs to be done over or differently?

1197. How much flexibility is there in the funding (e.g., what authorities does the program manager have to change to the specifics of the funding within the overall funding ceiling)?

1198. How timely were Progress Reports provided to the Customer Information Control System project Manager by Team Members?

1199. Who managed most of the communication within the Customer Information Control System project?

1200. How useful do individuals find communications?

1201. What is the quality and content of

communication?

1202. What are your lessons learned that you will keep in mind for the next Customer Information Control System project you participate in?

1203. How much communication is socially oriented?

1204. What is the frequency of communication?

1205. How do security constraints impact the case?

1206. Were any objectives unmet?

1207. How did the estimated Customer Information Control System project Budget compare with the total actual expenditures?

1208. Is your organization willing to expose problems or mistakes for the betterment of the collective whole, and can you do this in a way that does not intimidate employees or workers?

1209. How well is the build process working?

1210. How well were Customer Information Control System project issues communicated throughout your involvement in the Customer Information Control System project?

1211. How satisfied are you with your involvement in the development and/or review of the Customer Information Control System project Scope during Customer Information Control System project Initiation and Planning?

Index

Although   133
always 10, 260
ambiguous   238
ambitious   238
amended   155, 159
amount   24, 247, 260
amounts   234
amplify 65, 115
analysis   3, 7, 10-11, 46, 48, 55-56, 60, 66, 69-71, 81, 84, 89,
138, 143, 145-147, 173-174, 184, 186-187, 190, 202, 206, 210, 214-
215, 237, 247
analytics   57
analyze   2, 60, 62, 74, 207, 264
analyzed   56, 102, 145, 147, 194, 209
annual 186
annually   158
another   156
answer 11-12, 16, 28, 44, 60, 76, 93, 106, 225
answered   27, 43, 58, 75, 92, 105, 131
answering   11, 253
anyone   38, 108, 114
anything   162, 171, 174, 228-229
appear   1
applicable   12, 94, 149, 179, 195, 251, 253, 265
applied   84, 96, 205
applying   251
appointed   33, 38
appreciate   197
approach   57, 78, 86, 121, 126, 217, 223, 237-238, 245-246
approaches   82, 200-201
approval   34, 125, 162, 235
approvals   154
approve   147
approved   36, 68, 147, 150, 186, 199, 226-227, 259
approvers   147
approving   150
Architects   8
archived   181
archives   262
around 108, 121, 195, 237
articulate   218, 238, 246
asking 1, 8
assess   25, 34, 78, 96, 106, 170, 225

conform 154
connected 179
connecting 122
consider 17, 21, 23
considered 20, 22, 45, 190, 214, 228-229
considers 69
consist 195
consistent 42, 53, 69, 95, 195, 231, 245-246, 248
consortium 208
constantly 201
Constraint 3, 154, 252
consultant 8
consulted 129
consulting 57
consumers 120
contact 8, 144, 181, 198, 216
contain 26, 66, 99, 142
contained 1
contains 9
content 42, 215, 228, 266
contents 1-2, 9
context 31, 35, 37
continual 99, 104
continuity 44
continuous 72, 84
contract 7, 158-159, 169, 198, 223, 234, 259-260, 262-263
contracted 182
contractor 7, 153, 159, 215, 253, 260
contracts 34, 66, 138, 167, 180, 199, 212, 253, 259, 262
contribute 141, 148, 265
Control1-7, 9-14, 16-23, 25-33, 35-142, 144-150, 152-156, 158, 160-165, 167, 169-188, 190, 192, 194-200, 202-204, 206-210, 212-214, 216-228, 230, 233-235, 237, 239, 241, 243-251, 253, 255-260, 262, 264-267
controlled 73, 158, 265
controls 26, 72, 78, 81, 91, 94, 96-97, 99, 102, 104, 204-205, 259-261
convention 124
convey 1
cooperate 184
Copyright 1
corporate 231
correct44, 93

margin 162

market 21, 139, 221, 238, 249, 260

marketer   8

marketing   120, 167, 188, 264

markets   18

material   158-159, 167, 215, 247-248, 251

materials   1

matrices   150

Matrix 3, 5, 138, 150, 194, 208

matter 34, 51

maximize   231

maximizing   117

meaning   236

meaningful   55, 122, 158-159

measurable   33, 38, 239

measure   2, 10, 22, 25, 38-39, 44-47, 50, 52-56, 67, 70, 76-77, 82-83, 85, 91, 96, 100, 102, 139, 141, 184, 189, 237

measured   18, 45, 47-48, 50, 52-55, 90, 98, 103, 210, 245

measures   45, 51-52, 55-56, 58, 64, 70, 73, 80, 100-101, 103, 141, 192, 205, 210, 225, 240, 251

measuring   99, 158

mechanical   1

mechanics   224

mechanism   265

mechanisms   141, 193

medium   249

meeting   40, 95, 133, 193, 198, 201, 222, 229, 235-236, 252

meetings   33, 38, 43, 133, 152, 212

megatrends   126

member   6, 30, 109, 121, 172, 215, 222, 236, 239, 241, 245

members   30, 35, 43, 68, 100, 140, 175, 201, 212, 224, 233, 235-241, 245-246, 251-252, 266

membership   237-238

memory   225

Mentally   147

mentors   208

message   97, 218

method   48, 166, 237

methods   34, 37, 57, 71, 159, 180, 184, 202, 207, 214

metrics 5, 28, 63, 104, 155, 183, 190-191

milestone   4, 167, 170, 174, 186, 213

milestones   31, 137, 198, 247

minimize   134

requested   1, 84, 186, 226
requests   224
require 58, 68, 72, 95-96, 136, 159, 171, 206, 246
required   17, 21, 28-29, 31, 34, 37, 42, 54, 62, 66, 77, 82,
100, 133-134, 155, 164-165, 177, 190, 200, 205-206, 217, 219, 236,
264
requires   215
requiring   137, 263
research   21, 126-127, 167, 235, 239
resemble   221
reserve 159
reserved   1
reserves   199
reside   79, 162, 236
resolution   63, 85
resolve 17, 21, 25
resolved   220
resource   4-5, 126, 145-146, 171-173, 198-199, 221, 223
resources   2, 8, 20, 22, 24, 32, 42, 44, 64, 82, 100, 104, 113,
120, 126, 128, 135, 138, 141, 154, 164-165, 169, 173-174, 181, 185,
212, 217, 221, 239, 241, 244, 246, 265
respect   1
respond   141, 235
responded   12
response   20-21, 95, 97, 99, 101, 214, 253
responses   122, 204
responsive   176, 185
result   74, 89-90, 182, 184, 186, 190, 200, 226, 238, 263-264
resulted   102
resulting   63, 143
results 9, 32, 36, 57, 73, 76, 79, 82-83, 86-89, 100, 103, 141, 159,
166, 185, 190, 213, 221, 232, 239-240, 243, 251
Retain 106
retained   67
retention   53
retrospect   126
return   89, 111, 169, 188
revenue   20, 52
review 10, 29, 54, 62, 142, 212, 216, 225, 229, 235, 267
reviewed   38
reviews159, 162, 188, 202-203, 213
revised 74, 102
revisions   263

Lightning Source UK Ltd.
Milton Keynes UK
UKHW021031010620
364249UK00002B/178